MW00415270

RECONCILED

"A Story of Hope"

by Carl Gove

Copyright © 2019 Carl Gove
All rights reserved.

CONTENTS

PROLOGUE

2 Corinthians 5:20 "... be ye reconciled to God"

This book has been in my heart for many years now, since the events occurred. It is an account of personal experience, of a time in my life that was concurrently, in Dickens' words, " the best of times and the worst of times".

It is about my wife and myself, our relationship, its failures and triumphs. Obviously, I could not have written it without her. I'm so thankful for her. There's another person, without whom our story could not be told. I will introduce you to him in the telling. My mom has been after me for years to do this also, and a son cannot ignore the wishes of a mother.

I write with the greatest of gratitude. I have seen good, from a source I had not reckoned with, worked into my life through what you are about to read. My wish is that this source of goodness might cause hope to spring in you.

I realize that, for many struggling in this life, goodness is a rare commodity. I make no claims of possessing character that qualified me to be the recipient of anything in this regard. I had gone the way of all men in my short life, my weakness was my most apparent characteristic. The source I had not reckoned with had much to give, of which I was a receiver.

CHAPTER 1-"A DARK DAY"

The sky was that steel-gray color that thrusts all your thoughts inward, that made any depression a little deeper, any sadness a little more painful. My sadness and depression were already deep enough and I hated the gray gloom of the day that added to it, as if creation itself was in agreement with my condition. There was no escape and I was looking for one.

The ground was damp and clung to my insides. I lay on my back, just looking at the unyielding sky. It was empty, I was empty. Could I take my life? I looked at the bottle of pills and wondered if they would even work. Would it be quiet, would it be painful? Too much thought on the subject already. I really didn't want to do this. To stop and think about it is a return to living.

I got up slowly. Tears streamed down my face. I looked back and up at the window of the apartment where I knew she was. Maybe I hoped she saw me there, maybe I hoped she knew my thoughts and would rush to save me and us. The last weeks were so jumbled and confused. I was going from one emotion to the next without direction.

CHAPTER 2 –"THE FIRST TIME EVER I SAW HER FACE"

Six years earlier.   The rain of the afternoon was turning into snow as night came on and the temperature dropped. Jack and I got to the company Christmas party late. Everyone was there already, all our friends from work. It was a good group of people, we were all young and had a lot of fun when we got together. The party was at a country club out in Longmeadow, a ritzy suburb of Springfield. I didn't have a girlfriend at the time, neither did Jack. We were roommates in an apartment in West Springfield, close by work.

We sat down at the table. Everyone knew everyone. I sat across from Joanne. She and I were friendly with each other, worked on the same lines often. In fact we hired in on the same day, sat next to each other in the employment office. I had had a long talk with her mom that morning. She also was coming to work at Breck's, but Joanne and I hardly said a word. Her Mom had introduced us and that was it. Since then, we hadn't said much more to each other, but we were friendly.

I was pretty much done with my meal.   The band

had begun to play, not so well. Dance bands in the sixties had a tough time of it. It was a time warp for those kinds of bands. You couldn't dance to a lot of the music of the day. It was to be thought about. The lyrics were a revolution in themselves. A whole culture identified with them. We dressed different and thought different. So entertainment bands of this era either played music from the fifties or they played "Yesterday" over and over or tried to play contemporary, looking sadly out of place in their tuxes, cleanshaven and short-haired. When the eighties came along, dance music came back with a vengeance called "disco". If this band lasted that long, which I'm sure they didn't, they might have done better then.

I hadn't even thought of dancing. I was unattached and open to whatever might happen, but not necessarily looking for anything to. I was playing with the dessert on my plate. I looked up and across at Joanne. At the same time she looked at me. Her eyes were beautiful, a deep brown color, you could swim in them. Her long, dark hair picture-framed her pretty olive-skinned features. She looked beautiful, like I had never seen her before. She had on a white dress with a pattern of tiny roses on it. We smiled at each other and I heard myself asking her to dance.

We floated through a dance or two, not because I was a great dancer, we were just caught up in something we both were feeling. We kept looking into each other's eyes. I kissed her. I held her close.

Suddenly the universe revolved about her.

CHAPTER 3-"A DIAMOND IS FOEVER"

A week and a half later. "Will you marry me?"

"Yes."

I gave her a diamond. She loved it. I said, "Well, it's yours." Actually, it still belonged to the jeweler and some finance company for the next eight months.

CHAPTER 4-"BROKEN PLANS"

Joanne wanted to talk to me after work. Wanted to go to the park. The wedding was two days away.

We drove over to Forest Park, Springfield's green belt, where all the hippies hung out. We parked and walked into the woods a short distance and sat on a hill overlooking the outdoor amphitheater. The day was warm and sunny, a first sign of spring. There was no snow on the ground.

She started to cry. I knew what was coming. "I can 't marry you "

"Why?"

"I'm not sure it will last, I want to know it will. I'm afraid that in five years we'll want a divorce. I don't want to go through what my mom and dad went through and God help us if there's kids then."

She had legitimate concerns. For my part, I was devastated. Kind of selfish, not thinking about kids, just how I felt. I had had two serious relationships in my young life, one in high school, one while I was in college. I did not take breaking up very well. Because of that, with my other girlfriends, I destroyed any possibility of reconciliation. I couldn't let go. When this happened with Joanne, I thought to myself, "three strikes and you're out". I didn't know if I'd recover from this one.

We were still seeing each other every day at work. The first weeks after the shipwreck, I played the macho "I can take it, I don't really care" routine. Tried to act like nothing was happening. That wasn't me, it wasn't honest. I eventually just told her I loved her and I'd be there. It was up to her.

CHAPTER 5-"COMMITTMENT"

Johnny Cash did a weekly variety show on television for a short time in the sixties. He was country, but he had a place in his soul for contemporary artists too.

This Saturday night, Bob Dylan was to be a guest on his show. This was a cultural event for long-hairs. Dylan had dropped out of sight and sound for some time, reputed to be shut away in his home somewhere in upper New York state. This was his first public appearance in years. If anyone was a spokesman for the revolution of the sixties, Dylan was. The "Woodstock nation" was all in attendance on TV sets across the land. For the moment we would lay aside our aversion to twentieth century desensitizing technology and watch TV. This was Bob Dylan, our great high priest. We were all dutifully prepared, primed on the drug of our choice, our oblation and offering at the altar of worship. I was certainly one of his disciples and waited with great anticipation the event.

Joanne was with me. The marriage didn't happen in March and we had had some rocky going, but we were still seeing each other and talking about our relationship and the future from time to time. We were lying on a couch together, watching and waiting. Jack, Ray, Brenda, all our friends were there. The service was about to begin.

He sang a song with Johnny Cash that was on a current album, a ballad called "Girl From the North Country". He was so short and skinny. My idol was really just flesh and blood. I could never say it to anyone, but I was deeply disappointed that night. How could a troubadour of all that was right be so human, wasn't he supposed to be six feet tall with that faraway look in his eyes? I couldn't talk about it afterward. We just lay on the couch in silence for a time.

The room had emptied, people moving to different parts of the house. We didn't really notice. We were still lying on the couch, half sleeping, in each other's arms. We were chit-chatting about nothing for a time, then the conversation got more serious. We started talking about whether we would get married or not. As I said, we had approached this subject on occasion before, but with caution. Joanne needed time to make up her mind and test our love, so to speak. We talked of these things quietly, almost sleepily. It was now past midnight, the house was quiet, we didn't know where anyone was, but it didn't really concern us.

"We don't have to go the route of your parents, our marriage can be different," I said.

"How do you know that?"

"We commit to make it different. We decide not to let that happen, to stay together no matter what."

"We may not feel the way we do now in a few years."

"Everyone must go through that. It still comes down to a decision, to stay or leave. We've got to will to stay together, that's what marriage vows are about."

The conversation continued in this vein for a while longer. Somehow, I felt she was reassured by my words. She fell asleep beside me that night, her head on my shoulder. I thought about what I had said. It was the right thing. I knew it. It was what I wanted to give her, that kind of commitment. But where did those thoughts come from? They surprised me, that I could say something like that. I was twenty-one, unwise, to be sure, in the ways of life. Yet somehow that night I had touched on something that would never change. I had talked about love in an unpremeditated way with an air of confidence, as if I was an authority on the subject and had known these things all my life, that they were the truth.

There was a clarity in my mind as I lay there, before drifting off to sleep. I felt as if things were going to work out for us, if we did what we had just talked about. There was a rightness in what was said that had nothing to do with me or her or any couple struggling to stay together. It was just so.

CHAPTER 6-"THE WEDDING"

It was a beautiful September day, the sun shining brightly. I stood outside the wedding chapel and looked up and down the street at the cars passing by. The chapel was part of a big church, all stone and masonry, as much like a cathedral as anything you'd see in the States. My mom and dad had been married in that same chapel thirty-five years before. I had grown up going to church there every Sunday until I left high school.

I wondered if Joanne would change her mind again and not show up. I really didn't think so this time, but in the back of my mind an uneasy, lingering doubt was still there. I breathed a sigh of relief when I saw her coming up the long walk in her white mini-dress with flowers in her hair.

I remember how we looked at each other during the ceremony. I remember the promises we made. Some poetry was read, some great thoughts about love were espoused, most importantly though, we vowed to stay with each other forever. We left the chapel to the sounds of the Beatles' "All You Need is Love". People who were there said that there was something special about our wedding. It was a celebration. Our love had *been tested and stood up. People who knew us drew something from that fact. The growing strength of our relationship seemed to be contagious. There were genuine feelings of hope and happiness and good will we all felt throughout that day.*

CHAPTER 7-"A WHITE LIE"

It was a clear and windy day. Michelle's fourth birthday. I had put together a bike for her that morning. We would have a party later that day. I was taking the kids to the park down by the inlet. There were some swings there. They loved to swing and it was a beautiful day for it.

Michelle was on the swing, Keri was standing beside me. That's sort of the way my girls were. Michelle was the leader, the oldest by a year, always out in front. She loved life. She was physical and active, never holding back. Keri was quieter, content, willing to let her sister lead, not needing to be first. She was happy just to be there holding her daddy's hand

I watched Michelle as she swung out over the inlet. We were on a hill that sloped down to the water, so at the peak of the swing's motion, she looked poised over the water as if she could let go and drop straight in.

"Higher, daddy, higher!" Her eyes were wide with wonder and joy. She had huge round eyes, that looked like two full moons on her face. I remember when she was born and I saw her for the first time and those eyes looked up at me. She seemed to look through me

that day, as if to see who I really was. I've never forgotten that first look from my firstborn.

Keri was still beside me, smiling, holding my hand when she could. Her face was the picture of "pretty". She had the sweetest smile and the gentlest spirit to go with it. You couldn't easily get angry at Keri, she was so tender. The wind was chilly, so we finished our swings, got back in the car and headed home for the party.

"Daddy's going away for a while, going to work out of town."

They looked up at me quizzically. "You're coming back aren't you?"

"Oh sure, but I'll be gone for a little while though. You won't see me 'till I get back."

They seemed okay with that.

I had decided the day before to leave. It had been about a week since my aborted suicide attempt. My emotions were going crazy. I had pleaded a number of times with Joanne to reconsider this separation, but she had made up her mind. Wanting to let go and not make things worse, I thought the only way to do that would be to leave. I had such a hard time in the past when relationships broke down, I just couldn't see myself doing very well staying. I would probably drive the wedge that was between us deeper, until there was no hope for reconciliation. I thought to avoid that, the best thing to do would be to leave.

I felt a sense of relief actually in thinking about just walking away for the moment from all the hurt. I could go to Seattle and hook up with friends. "I'll just stay with them until I get work. I won't be dependent on them or wear out my welcome. Later I'll come back, maybe things will be different then." This train of thought had been the only bright spot in my thinking since all this had started.

CHAPTER 8-"HOPING AGAINST HOPE"

After the party, later that day, I told Joanne I had decided to leave. She didn't say much. I needed to pick up a check from the guy I'd been working with. Joanne decided to go with me to his house. We talked on the way over. She asked me where I would go. I told her. She wanted to know if I intended to come back.

"Yes, I still love you. I won't stay away from my kids forever. I don't really want to leave. You know I don't want any of this. Are you sure this is what you want?"

She sighed, "Yes, this hasn't happened overnight with me. Are you going to call Dwayne and Mary and tell them you're coming?"

"Yeah, I will on the way. I won't impose on them. Just 'till I get a job. I'm sure they'll help."

We pulled up to Ronny's house and sat in the car a few minutes in silence. I looked at her next to me, just a few feet away, yet, in our souls, miles apart. I could feel tears coming to my eyes.

"How did it come to this? Wasn't I a good husband?"

"It's not you. I got married too young. I'm twenty-

four years old with two kids. I feel like I missed something. I'm not happy anymore."

I couldn't listen to that without blaming myself. "I don't want this Joanne, what about the kids? They need me. "

"I know, but..." Her voice trailed away without finishing the thought.

I looked ahead, out the window of the car. There was a world out there, but I didn't know it. My world was confined to the front seat of my car. Everything that meant anything at that moment was there. I started thinking about God, which was strange. I hadn't really given him a thought in a long, long time. Without looking at her, really out of total frustration, I said, "I'm going to pray to God. He's the only one who can put this back together again." That was an incomprehensible thing for me to say. Probably just another attempt to elicit her sympathy. I had no thoughts for God, I didn't even know if he was real. Somehow, I guess I thought something out of the ordinary I could say or do would wake her up and she would suddenly just stop doing this and come back to me. Not so, not that day.

CHAPTER 9-"THE FAREWELL"

The girls were in bed. I had kissed each of them good-bye. I tried to hold back my emotions, wanting them to think I was just going away to work, something perfectly natural. I didn't know if that was how I should handle it, but it seemed right at the time.

They were asleep when I began putting the sum of my worldly possessions in my car. I was going through the motions like an automaton, numb, yet moving incessantly forward. That's so like humanity, striving just to survive. We can be in the most desperate of straits and yet we blindly continue going on, we don't know if for better or worse. We have to. I certainly was in that place tonight. My mind seemed emptied of thought. There was no sense to this. Just motion.

First my tools, then my clothes, not much in the way of belongings or personal items. A rifle that I never used, some books. Not much to show for the years of hard work, but I never gave possessions that much thought then anyway. My station wagon would be my home within the hour.

I was finished. I gave Joanne enough money to pay the current bills and buy food, gas, etc. She had plans to get a job. I promised her I would send money as soon as I got situated. There was little left to get to Seattle on, but I was going nonetheless. We stood in the living room looking at each other. There was tenderness still there. We hugged. She looked as though she was going to cry.

"I'll call when I get there. I love you. See you".

"Good-bye."

A kiss on the cheek.

It was a long walk down the two stories of stairs and out to the car. Seemed interminable. I was ready to turn around and go back at a word. Some part of me still hoped beyond hope I would hear that behind me, but it didn't come. She was standing in the window as I opened the door of the car and slid into the front seat. I looked up at her longingly. It was dark, so I couldn't see her face, just a silhouette framed against the light coming from the apartment. I backed out. My side of the car was to the apartment as I headed out. I looked up one last time. She was still there. I looked at my watch. It was exactly midnight. One day slipped into the next as I drove away, and I slipped into a whole different life. Tears came freely once again as I pulled out onto the highway heading north.

CHAPTER 10-"ON THE ROAD"

There is a single highway that runs north and south between the two major cities of mainland Alaska, Anchorage and Fairbanks. It is a road that stretches through vast expanses of untouched wilderness, from Ketchemak Bay in Homer, up the Kenai Peninsula to Anchorage, on along the foothills of the Alaska Range by Mt. McKinley, all the way to the edge of the Arctic Circle and the Brooks Range, beyond Fairbanks. This is no country road. When you leave Anchorage proper you are thrust into elemental nature. If your car breaks down, especially in winter, you are disconnected with the twentieth century and there is no town some short distance away that you could walk to. There's an unwritten law, especially in the winter, that if you see someone along one of the highways of the North, you must stop and see if they need you. This was summer though and I didn't need to worry about the cold. I headed toward the town of Palmer, a farming community in the middle of the famous Matanuska Valley, where potatoes and cabbages grow to sizes that would choke a large horse.

Summer is intense in the land of the midnight sun. It comes and goes quickly, three months long, between June and August. The days are long, the top of the planet, of which Alaska is a part, having rotated to a position where it practically looks into the full face of the sun. Night had fallen around eleven o'clock and daylight would come again at two in the morning.

I figured I would drive through the foreshortened night. Once I got to Palmer, about an hour and a half north, I would head east on the Alaska/Canada Highway toward the Yukon and Alberta and down into the lower forty-eight. Twenty-two hundred miles, and once into Canada, the last fifteen hundred on a gravel road.

I knew the road I was on well. We had made many trips out of Anchorage over the time we had been there. I probably knew it better than most. It was dark and I couldn't see a thing beyond what my headlights lit directly ahead of me. As the miles stretched between us, the sense of the reality of the separation began to set in. There was not going to be any turning back now. I was facing a completely unknown future. I never thought too much about risk in my life. I had somehow developed some kind of faith that things would work out for me. I had always been that way. Without that instinct, I guess I wouldn't have survived. Everybody must have that to some extent. I had ventured out of the comfortable in times past and always seemed to end up standing. I thought somehow this would be the same.

I was tired by the time I got to the other side of Palmer, where the highway began to climb up through a portion of the Chugach range. The trauma of finally leaving had left me emotionally drained. I thought I might fall asleep at the wheel. It was dark and the road was winding about. When I got to a straight section along a climb, I pulled onto the shoulder, cleared a place on my front seat and lay down to sleep. The sounds of the wilderness were discomfiting, because there were none. I had visions of a grizzly tearing open my door and me at the same time. I was tired though and eventually fell asleep. I looked forward to the daylight and the drive through the mountains. I thought I would find some comfort in their solitude and beauty.

It was not a peaceful sleep though. The AlCan is the only truck route between Alaska and the lower forty-eight states. Eighteen wheelers traveled it constantly, bringing in food and supplies to south-central Alaska and Fairbanks. Several times during my sleep one would pass by and throw gravel against the side of my car making enough noise to wake me. The car seemed to shake in the turbulence of the passing mobile monsters. I wondered if they could see me by the road. I slept intermittently for three or four hours, waking with the passing of each truck, wondering if I would become a hood ornament on the next one's front grill.

Sometime around five thirty in the morning I woke for the last time and headed out again. The day was sunny, but the beauty of nature's dawn couldn't overcome the general feeling of sorrow that seemed to be gaining an increasing grip on my soul. I passed by the Matanuska glacier, its icy fingers seemed to be reaching toward me as if to freeze me in my distress. I looked for the Dall sheep up along the slopes as I passed by Sheep Mountain. I remembered the spring of our first year in Alaska when Joanne and I and the kids had seen the ewes with their young grazing by the roadside. They were a majestic animal, so proud looking. Coming out of the mountains and into the open spaces of the tundra, I passed a lodge where we had stayed on that same trip for the night. We were a family then, it seemed so long ago. The lodge looked as empty and lifeless today as I knew my marriage was.

I reached the Canadian border just outside Tok and passed through without incident. You never knew what to expect at a border crossing. I was a scruffy looking guy and sometimes the Mounties just seemed to want to hassle you for no reason, but not today. As I left the stationhouse and pulled out on the road again, I could feel the hard gravel under my tires, digging into them like tiny spikes as I moved along. The Alaskan portion of the AlCan was paved, in Canada it wasn't, just dirt and gravel that turned into potholes and mud when it rained. I didn't want to think about my tires. They were in terrible shape. There was no way I would make it to Seattle on them and I didn't have the money to buy new ones. I was just hoping for the best, but I knew I had a problem. My spare would be no relief for the four miserable wheels that were supposed to take me two thousand miles over mostly unpaved highway. It would just be a matter of time now before they started giving out and passing air.

Sure enough, within the next hour, one corner of the car acted as if it was turning on a block instead of a wheel. I dragged out the spare, which looked like it could pass already for an inner tube. It had practically no tread left. I replaced it for the bad tire and gingerly headed down the road again, trying to avoid sharp pieces of gravel, which was difficult on an all-gravel road. When I reached a gas station, I went in and had the old tire repaired, put it back on in place of the spare, and tried again. Within three hours I was back in another gas station, repeating the same routine again. I would never make it out of Canada at this rate. My funds were limited and this was just aggravating the situation. I didn't know what else to do though, so I just kept plowing ahead.

That afternoon, two flat tires later, I picked up a couple of guys hitchhiking on the highway. They were heading to Haines, Alaska, a coastal town along the panhandle of the state, where they were going to catch a ferry south to Seattle. I told them I was driving to Seattle over the highway and I could take them as far as Haines Junction.

They were good company along the way. Helped me take my mind off of my circumstance. The remainder of the day was uneventful, no more flats to deal with, which gave me a false sense of hope of reaching Seattle *yet. Between the intermittent conversation, I looked out over the emptiness of the Yukon tundra, nothing more than a northern desert, just like the southern ones except that it's cold. In the distance you could begin to see the mountains of the Coastal Range. The day had become slightly overcast, which gave the north country that feeling it gets when it's gray, a feeling of loneliness, even desolation. Without the sun to give it color, the wilderness closed in on you, almost clamping down any uplifting emotions in your soul. I was glad for the conversation, when it picked up in the car. It took my thoughts away from the depressing landscape.*

We pulled into Haines Junction early in the evening, around ten thirty at night. It was just beginning to get dark. We stopped at a local restaurant for a hamburger and a beer and found out that an old church in the town was open at night, and we could sleep there if we wanted to. This was still the seventies, the era of the long-hair hippy. Local people in the states and Canada didn't have much sympathy for our philosophies, but it always amazed me how they would make provision for us nonetheless. Places like Alaska and Canada saw young transients passing through all the time during that period, male and female, young and old, good and bad. Out of some gut-level sense of kindness and charity, maybe because some of their own kids were out there somewhere, they made sure that if we came through their towns, we would have a place to stay out of the weather. There was even hot food and coffee at some of these hostels. I had taken advantage of places like these and of people like these before in my life. People's capacity to do things like this amazed me. It was a comfort to know they were out there, these givers of mercy. Tonight, it was an old wooden pew in an old wooden church in the Yukon. The night was cold, my bed was hard, but I had company around me and I slept well.

CHAPTER 11-"CHANGE
OF PLANS"

The following morning was the other face of the north country. The day sparkled in the morning sun. All of the colors of the approaching fall and the crispness of its attendant air coursed through my body and gave me a vitality I had not felt in some time. I was as changeable emotionally as the weather lately. As the day went, so did my soul. Today was bright and hopeful and it had its effect on me in the early morning hours.

My companions of the previous day were up too, and together we walked from the tiny old church, which had been our refuge for the night, to the main street of Haines Junction, the Yukon, Canada. We stopped in a small cafe and ordered coffee and breakfast.

"I guess this will be it for us," I said. "You're going south to Haines, I'm going east on the AlCan."

"You could come with us. We'll eventually get to Seattle," they offered.

"No, I can't, I don't have enough money for the ferry. I've got to get there with what I have and can't really

take my time." A fleeting picture of my bald tires rose like an uncomfortable specter in my mind. My money to get me to Seattle was in jeopardy and I knew it.

"My wife and kids are going to need money soon, I've got to get there and get settled quick."

"Yeah, I understand," ventured one of my riders. "It's been good traveling with you, you've brought us a long way."

"Hey, no problem, I needed the company"

We finished our breakfast and walked back to my car. I brought them as far as the junction and said my good-byes.

Driving off down the highway to the east, my company gone, already my thoughts began to crowd in on me again. But the beauty of the morning kept them from digging down too deep.

Heading out across more tundra, but with the sunshine and color, I noticed it had a different aspect than yesterday. I was driving through bare rolling hills, golden brown, with patches of green here and there and even some tiny wildflowers showing. Off in the distance were the mountains, their blue-gray rocky peaks jutting into the sky, snowcapped along the ridgeline, the last remains of the previous winter. The ribbon of road stretched out endlessly before me. I had come to Alaska two years before on that same road, but had forgotten where or how far it was to the next town or gas station. I had filled up when I got into Haines Junction the night before. I thought I had better look at the map and try to plan my day. I looked at the distance to Seattle. It was a long way. Seventeen hundred miles at least. If my money held out and got me there, I would be fortunate. I would be pretty dependent on Dwayne and Mary until I got work and a place. I never wanted that, I wanted to make my own way. They didn't even know I was coming, much less that they'd have to support me for a couple of weeks.

I thought to myself, "Twenty two hundred miles from Joanne and the kids. If I had to get back here quickly, how could I do it? That's too far away." To get to Alaska from the lower forty-eight is a major accomplishment, a task. Once you leave, it's another task to get back. They were still my family, even though we were separated. I had to stay closer than Seattle.

But where I wondered? I started looking at the map for an answer. Dawson Creek, Whitehorse, just outposts in the wilderness. I remembered how much I had liked British Columbia on the trip up here. Most of the country between me and the border was sparsely populated though, towns few and far between. Work would be hard to find. Outside of the stretch I went through on the AlCan two years ago, I knew nothing of it. I looked up from Vancouver, along the coast. Prince Rupert, maybe I could make it there. But I'd be trying to get work as an American in Canada. That would be a hassle. I would need a green card to be legal. Plus, the road to the coast, if there was one, went through the Coastal Range. It could be paved or it could be treacherous. Again, I just didn't know.

My eye wandered up the map along the coast. Ketchikan, Wrangell, Sitka. No roads to any of those places. Accessed by the ferry only. Further up, Juneau. Juneau, one ferry-stop from Haines. A small town, but the capitol of the state. There had to be some construction work there. It was still the U.S., I could work there without worrying about citizenship. One ferrystop to a road that could get me back to Anchorage, eight hundred miles versus two thousand. I'd have plenty of money to get there and probably enough to tide me over 'till I got a job. My heart leapt at the thought of this. I always wanted to go there, ever since I'd been in the state. Coastal fjords, the waterway, logging country, evergreens, glaciers. It seemed perfect. I would still be in Alaska and could get back home if things changed.

My whole spirit was lifted by this change of plans. I tried to calm myself down and think through it again, but I had already made my decision. I was elated. Everything was still an unknown, but somehow this seemed right. I hurriedly folded up my map, got back in my car and headed back the few miles I had driven from Haines Junction. I tried to drive with some caution, my tires were still as bald as an eagle's crown, but I was speeding over the gravel road, spewing tiny rocks in all directions, like one of those eighteen wheelers always driving through. When I got to the junction, I turned to the south and headed for Haines, the ferry, and on to Juneau. I was flying in more ways than one, my car was and my mind was too. Optimism prevailed. I had a fresh hope that things might fall into place and I would still be in touch with home. I would be in Haines that afternoon. I remember my riders from yesterday mentioning the ferry for Juneau would be leaving that night about ten o'clock. They'd be surprised to see me on board. Perfect, I'd be in Juneau that night. Tomorrow was Monday and I would start settling in there and looking for work. This was going to be okay. I was breathing a little deeper now and relaxing a bit. I would enjoy the rest of the day, everything was settled now.

CHAPTER 12-"A
MEMORABLE DRIVE"

I felt good, I was up. My fresh resolve, having breathed new life into me, was carrying me along my way. For the first time in weeks, my mind was off of Joanne and our problems. I knew that would not be a permanent state, but I would enjoy it while it lasted. It was mid-morning now and the sun shone brilliantly overhead in a cloudless sky.

A short way out of Haines Junction I reunited with my riding companions from yesterday. The whole process of deciding to retrace my route and head south really hadn't taken all that long and they had not found a ride yet. I pulled over to pick them up again. They were surprised.

"What's this? What are you doing here? Decide to go with us?" they asked.

"No, I'm going to Juneau. Makes more sense for me for a lot of reasons," and I began to explain my change of plans to them.

"Yeah, I think you're doing the right thing. Better to be up here where you can get back home," one replied.

"That's one of the main reasons. I don't know what

will happen with all this yet. I may have to go back or she may want me to. Anyway, I'll be on that ferry with you tonight."

Our mutual destination and plan for the day decided, we settled into a relaxed driving mode and began to really take in the terrain along the way. We were steadily climbing into the foothills of the Coastal Range, a ridge of mountains that separated the narrow coastline along the panhandle of Alaska from the main body of Canada. These rugged mountains were part of the history of this place. They were a formidable obstacle to the fortune hunters that swarmed up here in the great Klondike gold rush days.

The mountain peaks were closing in on us. We were passing through high tundra, still golden brown under the bright sunshine. The perpetual patches of snow could be seen higher up where the rocky summits cut their jagged patterns against the sky. We were heading toward a pass which would take us over the summit of the range and then down to the coast on the other side.

We kept climbing through open country until we entered the pass, a high mountain valley with a row of peaks on both sides of the road. The road was straight and level for about three miles. We were driving very close to the peaks we had seen at a distance a short time ago. If you pulled to the side of the road, you could easily climb on either side to any number of summits.

We stopped for a short rest from the driving and walked part way up one of the slopes and sat, just taking in the view, snow-capped summits against the blue sky. Getting back in the car we moved on. As soon as we came through the pass we began a winding descent.

Being on the coast side now, due to the increased amount of rainfall and snow captured on the west-facing slopes of the range, the high meadows had turned green and the gray rocky portions below the peaks looked smooth from the constant runoff of moisture. The snow reaching down like fingers from the peaks was clean and white. The three of us were really caught up in the beauty of it all as we drove along. We continued, descending away from the high ground of the pass, and as we came around a few more bends we could see the tree line below us. The growth was not scrub brush like on the tundra side we had left. These were real trees. Evergreens, mostly spruce, tall trees with thick round trunks. We began to see signs of logging as we descended into the forest, piles of decaying sawdust lying by makeshift mills. The operations consisted of a building or two, canopy-like wooden structures covering a rip saw and piles of rough-sawn lumber. There was no sign of activity. The buildings set up around the saws didn't look like houses of any sort, more like places to store tools and equipment.

We passed through the Alaskan border checkpoint

just after entering the forest, a guard post with two agents on duty, an American and Canadian. The American agent practically waved us through, after checking our citizenship. Since we were all Americans, there was nothing more he cared about, we were coming home. At the other door of the post, the Canadian agent checked the cars coming out of Alaska in the opposite direction.

The road kept on its steady descent down the mountainside through the evergreen forests. With the bright sun beaming down through the branches of the lofty trees, the forest had the enchanting look of a natural cathedral. Patchworks of rust-brown color shone on the forest floor, strewn with a carpet of fallen needles and cones. A number of slain tree-giants could be seen laying prostrate across the ground. How the mighty had fallen no one knew, whether from a storm or by the hand of the sawyer. A delicate covering of emerald green moss had begun to grow over some like a grave cloth, and you envisioned years from now that the forest would simply swallow up its heroes, and a mound upon the ground would tell the future a great tree had died there, nature's cemetery markers to its lost sentinels.

As we continued on, birch and alder and poplar trees began to mix with the thinning stands of spruce. Eventually they dominated the landscape, their increasing size telling us we were close to being down the mountain and onto the floor of the valley below. Marshy areas indicated that a river was close by and soon the road was following a course along its bank, taking advantage of the path it had cut through the trees centuries before us all. The number of trees continued to decrease as we passed by sections of the river that widened out increasingly before us. Soon we were driving again through open spaces, a ridge of mountains to the north, covered with thick forests of spruce from the foothills to the tree-line where rock walls continued up to the snow of the peaks. We had just traversed that same terrain on our way over the pass. The river stretched off to the west, wide and flowing steadily on its course to the sea.

Off in the distance a delta stretched out where this river and others, tumbling out of the range from points north, emptied their alluvial deposits of silt and sand by the open mouth of the sea. Tucked between the mountains and the estuary was the town of Haines, spread over and around the wide ocean bay that mingled the fresh water of the rivers with the sea. To the west, the bay funneled its contents into the Inside Passage, a vast collection of waterways, glacial fjords and forested islands that comprised the Alaskan coast from here to Ketchikan in the south. This dynamic of land and water and the beauty it had created had been established, in some way I knew not of, from the very beginnings of time. It had all been set into motion by some unseen force, natural or otherwise. We were that day the recipients of nature's artwork of the ages.

CHAPTER 13-"HAINES, ALASKA"

On the last leg of our trip into Haines we passed by a logging mill. Logging and fishing were the main industries in the town. It was also a ferry stop for the Alaskan State Ferry, which serviced the coastal towns from Haines to Seattle. Besides the mill, there was a canning factory a short distance outside the town on the bay, and a nice hotel for tourists up on a hill that overlooked the business center of the town. The hotel was a converted post commander's quarters. There used to be an Army post there during and after the Second World War. It looked like a stately southern manor, its large porch looking out on what used to be a parade field. Around the field were a number of residences, small and sturdy, plain-faced, perhaps former post quarters, with steep roofs to dump the abundant snow load they would see in winter. In a corner of the field stood a small church that overlooked the bay. The grass of the field was a lush late-summer green and the temperature was quite warm. From the height of the parade field the roads to the town below all twisted down a steep slope. Like many military facilities, this one was built on a precipice above the fray. The men who had been quartered there had a place away from the normal rush of life. The area still had that feeling of being set apart from the rest of the town, isolated, in a sense, for some other purpose. It served well as a place for travelers, which, because of the ferry, Haines saw a lot of. Here was a place to maintain that distance a traveler feels from the local population, a retreat where one doesn't need to get sullied with the life in the town below, where you could pass through and observe and touch only if you chose to do so.

For the first time in my life I saw, on the way into town, an American bald eagle. Being American, it was, for me, a special event. Haines and its estuary were a mating ground for these birds, and they could be seen year-round in and around the town. The eagle, bald or otherwise, is the most majestic of birds, stately and proud. One could be hypnotized just watching them in flight, rising on the wind currents above the forests of the foothills, gliding up and up, ever watchful of the minutest movement below, ready to swoop down in a moment upon some unsuspecting prey, or just sitting upon the highest branch of a spruce or birch, chest out, head high but still watching, both on guard and ready to attack at the same time.

When we reached the town, we headed straight for the local bar for some refreshment of the inebriating type. This establishment was Alaskan to the core, a large log structure with wood everywhere, on the bar, pool tables, benches, chairs, tables, even the toilet seats. In spite of the dark look of the wood, it was still bright inside, with the afternoon light from the west shining through its front windows. A sit-down restaurant was off to the left as you entered the door, separated from the main room, which contained the bar and pool tables, where everyone was today. It was crowded, most of the people travelers, waiting for the ferry to come and take them away that night, stopping here only for a drink along the way. The crowd was a young one,

Alaska attracted youth, individuals full of dreams and willing to risk something to see them fulfilled, coming to a land that was not without a reputation for testing your resolve. Many of the people in the state at this time were heading north to the pipeline camps, to work on the construction crews and save their money, hopefully. If they could avoid the temptations that came with the camps and their big paychecks, they could return to the lower forty-eight in a year or two with a stake.

The three of us took seats at the bar and ordered beers. I turned around and leaned back against the edge of the bar, drink in hand, and relaxed, looking around at the company I kept.

The atmosphere of the place was high, people drinking and laughing and looking generally happy about life, unusual for a bar, but the sun was still traveling through the course of one of its more beautiful, clear days and if people were anything like me, their moods often swung with the weather, from happy to sad as the sun came and went. It was just *mid-afternoon, so spirits were still up.*

I thought as I looked around at the animated crowd, that I was a free man now, I could play the field if I wanted to and seeing a pretty brunette across the room, I wondered if that wasn't what I did want to do. This was the sixties, the days of liberation. I was still thinking of my wife. I loved her, but thoughts of fidelity sometimes had little part in our moral code of the day, which, when I think of it now, was really short of anything you could call moral. As the words of a popular song of the day expressed it "when you can't be with the one you love, love the one you're with".

I finished my beer and left those thoughts and turning to my companions, I inquired, "Do you want to take a walk with me around the town?"

"No, we 'll stay here. Look for us when you come back. "

"All right, I won't be long."

Across the street, were the town barber shop, a craft store, a hotel and further along I could see some buildings that looked like the type you would see in a fishing town, boat repair shops, bait and tackle shops, a seafood restaurant, a coffee shop, another bar, this one much more local looking, probably a hangout for fishermen and loggers from the area. I turned right when I got to Main Street and continued my walk. The town was so small and picturesque, like something you'd see in a postcard. It reminded me of places I'd seen back home in Maine or at Cape Cod, little shops that provided all of the necessities that supported life for the fifteen hundred or so people that populated Haines, tourist places selling Indian jewelry, painted gold pans, woodcarvings, all of them creations that represented the people and history of this place.

Coming to the comer of a small tree-lined side street that ran into Main I looked into a restaurant there. It was your typical breakfast, lunch and five-dollar dinners' working man's place. Being a carpenter, I'd been to nearly all these places in southcentral Alaska around Anchorage and feeling right at home, I went in, thinking I'd eat some lunch now, then not eat again 'til I got on the ferry that night. I ordered a salad and hamburger plate with coffee from the waitress, took a seat by the window, inhaled the whole meal in one breath, which was my usual hurried way of eating, checked my bill to remember what I ate, then sat back and relaxed while I drank my cup of coffee. My thoughts seemed to be flying through my mind so fast I couldn't catch any to collect, so I finished my coffee, paid my bill and resumed my walk, which seemed the only thing to do with this restlessness which had come upon me from who knows where.

I headed up the side street, figuring to circle my way back around to the bar at the other end of it. This was a residential street, but not like any you would see in the lower forty-eight. A row of houses to my left could be seen, but immediately behind them was thick forest, not the backyards of neighbors and more streets of homes. This was small-town Alaska, where every street away from the main drag looked, in some way or other, to be on the edge of the town. In any direction, a short drive or walk would bring you into rugged wilderness. The nearest town to the north was Haines Junction, where I started from that morning. It was a hundred miles, back over the coastal range, into Canada. To the south was Juneau, but the road ended in Haines, and the only way to get to there was by the ferries. West was the Waterway and the open ocean of the Gulf of Alaska and north was miles of deserted coastline which stretched all the way to the Kenai Peninsula and the shores of Cook Inlet, where Anchorage was, but few commercial boats and no ferries ventured north from Haines, too far and too treacherous along the shores of the Gulf.

As I walked along I noticed signs of new construction. A freshly poured foundation was tucked into a clearing in the trees to my left, next to it another one and I could see a crew doing finish work on a third further up the street. I kept looking along that side and noticed two more foundations, one just recently poured and then finally a fifth, with what to a framing carpenter was the holy grail, a bare slab with a pile of lumber stacked in front of it. I immediately thought, "Work, where's the framers?" I looked again at the three-man crew working on the middle foundation of the five which lined the street. I headed toward them, thinking I would inquire about the houses.

"Hi, is one of you the contractor or know where I could find him?"

A man, probably in his thirties, six-foot, black-haired, with glasses and a short, but thick, black mustache came up to me and introduced himself.

"I'm Asbjorn Bo," he said in a thick Scandinavian accent, removing his work glove and extending a sand-paper rough working man 's hand toward me, "People call me Bo. I'm building these houses." He had a bright, cheerful look, the sides of his mouth turned slightly upward, as if he wanted to break into a grin or a smile at the first opportunity. This was not the normal look of the men I had grown used to in Alaska. Most of them were fiercely competitive individuals and had that hard, preoccupied look, suspect of everything and everyone around them, gaging you, measuring you, always feeling you out. This man was different, seemingly trusting and trustworthy at the same time. He drew me into the conversation with his sincere friendly manner.

"I'm a carpenter," I ventured, "a framer."

"Yes?" He replied, in a tone that seemed interested and wanted to know more.

"I've had my own business in Anchorage. I'm on my way to Juneau to look for work. Do you have framers for these houses or are you doing them yourself? "

"I'm from Juneau. I had a crew lined up. They were going to come up here this weekend and start that house up the street tomorrow. They called me today and said they wouldn't be coming. Decided to take another job in Juneau."

"Sounds like you might need some help."

"Yes, it looks that way. One of the men working with me has done some carpentry work, but he couldn't frame by himself, and I need to go back and forth some to Juneau. My family's there and I have other jobs there also. I bought these lots as spec lots. Want to build the houses and sell them myself."

"I don't need to go to Juneau if I could work here. Maybe I could work something out with you by the hour. I could run your framing. That's what I do."

"What would you need?"

I thought about it. Ten dollars cash, would that be too high? I could make it on a little less. "Eight dollars cash would work for me." This was an offer I didn't think he could refuse, it was actually pretty cheap.

"That sounds reasonable," Bo replied. He probably was ready to break out in that grin he was always cheating towards at my offer. "When do you want to start?"

"In the morning. You'll have a framer there just like you planned."

"That's great." he said.

"Okay, I'll see you then "

"In the morning, seven o 'clock then." We shook hands to seal the deal and he headed away back to the foundation.

I turned back the way I had come. This was huge. I couldn't believe my good fortune. I had been in this town less than an hour and had a job framing five houses. I was still in Alaska and didn't have to do anything but get in my car and drive if I needed to get back to Anchorage. My head was swimming with thoughts. I went back into the restaurant where I had had lunch. I had said a couple of words to the owner when I was there.

"Hey," I exclaimed, "I just got a job from that guy building those houses up the street. Looks like I'll be here for a while, probably see you quite a bit for meals."

"Hey, that's good, "he replied, "that's real good Come by in the morning. We got good breakfasts."

"Yeah, I'll see you then."

I left the restaurant and headed back down Main Street. I turned to the right instead of going immediately back to the bar and walked down along a narrow stretch of beach that ran along the bay. I looked out over the bay, at the fishing boats resting on the calm waters, at the mountains across the way that rose abruptly from the edges of the shoreline. The trees, the eagles, this picture-postcard town was going to be home. All my life as a long-hair hippie I wanted to live in a place like this, remote, close to the natural elements, yet with enough people around to keep you from getting lonely. It was a dream I had when I came here from Massachusetts. How much had happened from this morning when I had decided to change course and go to Juneau? Here I was now, actually going to live in this beautiful place, with money in my pocket and a job to go to in the morning. I was overwhelmed. I could not remember having such a sense of good fortune in many years, not since I had met Joanne or had my kids. I didn't know how to take it at first. There was so much emotion welling up in me as I sat on the moorings of a dock and took in the sights around the bay. I'd get to know this place. I'd travel out of town on every road I didn't know, take the ferry to Juneau some weekend, go to Skagway, go back up to the pass in Canada and do some climbing. It would be great. I was really living here. I still couldn't believe it. I had to call Joanne and tell her. Wait 'til the guys I came here with hear this. I headed back happily toward the bar and a telephone. I would celebrate the rest of the day. What a day in the life!

CHAPTER 14-"NEW BEGINNING"

The phone call home was entirely uneventful and actually dampened the exuberance I was feeling just moments before. My enthusiasm about my good fortune was not contagious, Joanne seemed cold and distant. I had hoped to hear some hint in her tone of voice that would say, "I miss you, come home", but it just wasn't there. I wondered how her first days alone had been, what thoughts had crossed her mind, but we certainly weren't in a place in our relationship to talk of such things. The conversation was beginning to drain me, I did not want to go back to the gloominess that had pervaded my thoughts for so many days prior to this one. I ended the conversation quickly and headed back into the bar.

My traveling companions were much more willing to share my good fortune and we spent the remainder of the afternoon and evening in the bar, talking and drinking and getting pretty drunk by the time I brought them to the ferry at ten o'clock.

Being high on something had become a way of life for me. It was as if I needed some stimulation always in my system to put an edge on my existence, or dull my senses to it, whichever. Drug use had begun in my life as what I envisioned as a quest for enlightenment, but over the years, with little enlightenment to show for the effort, had sadly degenerated into escape and habit. I was generally, even before all the trouble in my marriage, growing increasingly unhappy and resigned. The youthful idealism of a few years past had given way to a bitter sort of cynicism about life and our ability to live above the normal planes of existence. I had settled into a routine of long hours of work and staying stoned on marijuana. I just wanted to get through each day without thinking too much about it. I remained in a perpetual daze that seemed to fit my inner disposition. The thought occurred to me that I wasn't able to be much help to Joanne in the state I was in. Somehow, I had never realized this when I was with her. I had become inward and preoccupied in a dismal sort of way. No wonder we had grown apart.

Marijuana was my drug of choice. I had smoked it pretty much constantly for the past six years. When I left Anchorage, I was without any, which was really unusual for me. Even being at the bar for the short time I was in Haines, I had asked around for some. I was told by a local dealer that the town was pretty dry at the time, but by the end of the week, he would have some for sale. So, I did the next best thing, I drank.

Later that night I headed with my friends to the ferry stop to drop them off. I said my final good-byes and headed slowly back the mile or two from the terminal to the town. I went back to the street where the foundations were and pulled into the driveway by the stack of lumber I had seen that afternoon, figuring that's where I would probably start work in the morning. I was going to sleep in my car again that night. It was still late summer and the nights were warm enough to get away with that now, though soon September would be here and the temperature would begin to drop, whether you were ready for it or not. I had enough money left to get me to my first paycheck next Friday. I had seen a small hotel across the street from the bar and would get a room there next weekend. That would be home.

As I lay my head down on the front seat, I contemplated my new life to be. The drinking had had its effect and my good mood had begun to wane. I had never been a heavy drinker and wondered if that would change now if pot wasn't readily available. I thought my life would be a routine of working, heading for the bar, drinking or smoking probably 'til late at night and finding my way across the street to my room. It all seemed rather dreary now. My head was heavy with drink and thoughts. What a change. A week ago I had a family to go home to. I thought of Michelle and Keri and wondered if they were missing me tonight. I could feel a loneliness creep into the car and begin to cover me like a morning fog might cloak the town and the bay, obscuring any sense of direction and pressing the immediacy of present circumstance upon me unceasingly. Where had that feeling of ebullience I felt that afternoon gone. I wanted to hold it longer and keep it near, but I couldn't as I faded off to sleep. It was fleeting away with the last thoughts of the day. I hoped tomorrow that hard work would be a therapy and keep me from going into the depression I felt coming on.

CHAPTER 15-"WORK"

I was up well before the dawn, anxious to get to work. I drove down the street to the restaurant I had been to the day before and ordered the usual Alaskan breakfast, eggs, bacon, hash browns and sourdough toast, with the ever-present cup of coffee. Not much distinctly Alaskan to it, except maybe the sourdough, but this had been my usual fare for as long as I'd been a carpenter in the north country.

I was comfortable in these restaurants. Tradesmen in all the towns and cities from Ketchikan to Fairbanks congregated in places like these. They were like the union halls of the independent contractors. I had gotten jobs over cups of coffee, and there was a sense of camaraderie there amongst the blue-collar clientele. The waitresses were "homey-looking" working girls (not what you"re thinking), many of them divorcees, sometimes attractive, but not often. They knew how to handle the men though. They were friendly, at a distance, and didn't blush at the sound of a four-letter word. You rarely saw many women in these establishments besides the waitresses.

I used the rest room to clean up and shave around the outlines of the beginnings of my growing winter beard. It was still early, and not many people had come into the restaurant yet. I finished my meal quickly and gulped down my coffee, still jumpy with anticipation about the coming day. At quarter to seven I headed back up the street to the house, where Bo was just coming out of a temporary trailer he was staying in on the property.

Bo and I hit it off right from the start. He was affable, an easy person to talk to, at least for me. He brought me a cup of coffee from the trailer and spread out a set of blueprints on the lumber pile. We looked them over and planned the day's work. I would start laying out the house that was ready to be framed while he finished up the foundation work on the other houses. He would use the carpenter he had hired to help him. He said he wanted to get another person to help me once I got a ways along. It appeared that he would be coming and going between here and his home in Juneau. Apparently he had a job he was finishing there. That suited me fine. I worked best on my own and it looked like I would call the shots on the framing, which is what he wanted. There never seemed to be any question in his mind about my ability, as if some kind of immediate trust had been established between us right from the start. He seemed very comfortable with the situation, even though I had just turned up on his job yesterday. I wondered about that. Most of the people I worked with tended to be distrustful and antagonistic, acting always as if you were trying to take something from them instead of trying to help them. Not so with Bo. I was not used to this, but I liked it nonetheless. He headed down the street to the foundations and left me to myself.

I pulled tools out of my car, hooked up my saws and began to cut and bolt down the sill plate for the first story. It felt good to be working. Framing was something I loved. Being out in the weather, seeing a building raised up, your progress visible at the end of each day. It was hard yet satisfying, work. The day began to warm up under a clear sky and my mind was absorbed in the house and my efforts to build it.

About an hour or so later, Bo came up the street with the other man who had been working with him yesterday afternoon. I assumed this was the carpenter he had mentioned then and again this morning.

"Carl, I'd like you to meet Wendell Terwilliger. He's helping me with the foundations. Wendell, Carl Gove, just into town yesterday. A framer. He came at the right time, with the crew from Juneau backing out at the last minute."

I shook hands with Wendell. He had a warm handshake and a very gentle demeanor. Again, not your usual Alaskan type. I began to think that maybe Southeastern was a lot different environment than the mainland up north.

"Wendell does carpentry only part time. He's the

pastor of the Baptist church up on the hill by the hotel. Have you seen it?"

I did remember seeing the little church on the edge of the parade field when I first drove into town yesterday. "Yeah, I think I went by it. It's the one by the big hotel, right?"

"That's it," Wendell said

So, he was a minister. "Bo must go to his church," I thought. Maybe this explained the gentle natures that emanated from these men. I left it at that.

"Nice to meet you.," I extended my hand to him again. "Guess we'll be working together."

They turned and headed back down the street and I returned to the floor joists. "Nice guys, church guys," I thought to myself again. "Hope they don't start preaching at me."

The rest of the day was rather uneventful. I was doing my thing, framing. I had become a good carpenter since coming to Alaska. I could drive a sixteen-penny nail with one or two swings of my thirty-two-ounce hammer and I was progressing at a good pace on the house. I knew Bo would be more than satisfied with what he saw at the end of the day. Around four-thirty, he came by.

"Good job, Carl, you'll work out fine. You can quit anytime now. I usually go about ten hours a day. You can do more if you want. I figure you should

work between fifty and sixty hours a week, six days. I usually don't work Sundays."

"That's fine. I plan on getting a room in the hotel over by the bar by the first of next week. Would you mind if I slept in my car on the property 'till then?"

"No, that's okay. Pull up anywhere you like. I'll see you tomorrow, same time, seven o'clock."

"Okay, sounds good"

Bo headed for his trailer and I for the bar. I had a good feeling about this guy and this job after the first day.

CHAPTER 16-"DRUNK"

I settled into my anticipated routine of working days and going to the bar at night. Tuesday night I had dinner at the restaurant that was adjacent to the bar. The waitress was a pretty blond girl, very attractive. Again, I thought of the possibilities of pursuing some kind of relationship with someone. I thought to myself, "I'm virtually unattached, maybe I could meet her." I wasn't sure if I was ready for anything like that. She was just good looking. My relationships with women tended to be always serious. Besides my wife, I had had my two serious girlfriends in high school and college. Of course, there were dates and all that along the way, but I was raised in a church and the thought back then that one could have a romance, including sex, was foreign to me. I still retained a bit of that upbringing, the old-fashioned opinion that sex meant you were serious about the person you were with, in spite of the fact that now I was a "liberated" hippie. I contemplated all this over a plate of oysters, coming to no conclusion on the matter. After eating, I headed into the bar for some drinks. It was quiet that night, not too many people there, so I went home early to my car and slept.

The following day was just like the last two, work,

something to eat and to the bar. Still no sign of any "pot". Thursday evening there was a pretty good crowd, a lot of customers on their way to the ferry which was leaving later that night, again at ten o'clock. I met a couple of guys from Canada, who were on their way to Vancouver and we got to drinking pretty heavy and decided after a time to bar hop around town and see if there was anything more lively going on somewhere else. I told them I had seen a bar down by the docks. We headed there, ordered a beer but didn't stay long. The locals did not look real friendly and we were getting louder with every beer we consumed. We left that place and headed for the big tourist hotel up on the parade field above the town. I was pretty loaded on beer by this time and was having trouble driving up the narrow streets. I remember passing by the church and seeing a parsonage that I hadn't noticed before tucked away behind it. There was a warm and inviting look to the house. I could see the lights shining from the rooms inside. I wondered if that was where Wendell lived? If he could see me now. We got to the hotel in one piece, drank 'till nine-thirty or so and headed back to the bar where we started from for one last drink. The Canadians headed for the ferry. I wondered how they would manage the winding road along the bay. I staggered back to my car, thoroughly drunk, wondering how I would manage three or four blocks to the jobsite. I found my way to one of the lots, where I parked and slouched down on the seat in a heap. I hadn't mixed drinks, so I wasn't going to be sick, but my head was spinning like a top. "Could I control this," I asked myself? I was afraid of becoming an alcoholic. I had never drank like this before in my life, night after night. Could I stop? I couldn't answer the questions. I fell into a deep sleep. If I dreamed, I don't remember any of it. I slept the sleep of the drunkard.

I woke up suddenly. It was broad daylight. I could hear voices. I propped myself up on my elbow and looked out. The crew was working on the foundation next to the one I was parked on. I looked at my watch. Nine-thirty in the morning.

"Oh, God!" I thought to myself. "Three days on this job and I'm late for work. What will Bo think? He probably knows I was drinking."

I sheepishly got out of the car, said "hello" to the crew and looked for Bo. I could see him up the street by the house I was supposed to be working on. I got back in the car and drove up to where he was. My head was pounding. I parked up beyond the lot, got out and started towards where he was standing, waiting for me. I was trying to rehearse my apology as I walked the few steps back down the road

"Good morning." No reply from him. He didn't look angry, but I knew it was still my turn to speak.

"I got drunk last night. I don't know what to say. I'm not an alcoholic, I don't want you to think that. This isn't like me." I was like a kid caught with his hand in the cookie jar, desperately making excuses to avoid a

spanking.

He looked almost tenderly, like a father at me. I remembered that yesterday, just before I left work, he had asked me to go to church with him that night. I had quickly said "no" and headed for the bar and my night of woe. Without really thinking about what I was saying I blurted out, "My wife and I just separated last week. She's in Anchorage with my kids, two little girls." I could feel tears coming. "I'm having a bad time of it, really struggling."

I was not trying to just excuse myself with this talk. It was coming from my heart. The next thing that came from my mouth was a total surprise to me. He had still not said a word, he was looking straight at me and listening.

"Would you pray for us? We need it." I felt a tear coming and one fell slowly down my cheek. I was embarrassed, I didn't want to cry in front of him.

Bo unbuckled his nail bag, let it just fall on the ground beside him, and finally spoke, "Come into the trailer, we'll pray right now." He began walking ahead of me, I followed. We went inside. It was a small twenty-foot trailer, bunks in the back, a living area and a kitchen/dining area in the front, all one room, except for a bar-type divider between the kitchen and the living room. We sat at a small dinette in the kitchen. I was uncomfortable. It had been years since I had said a prayer. He bowed his head and began. I didn't really hear a word. I just sat where

I was and leaned forward in an appropriate posture, my elbows on my knees, my head in my hands, trying to hold back tears that wanted to flow. I could hear him still praying, but I still wasn't listening to the words. I was full of emotion, but nearly void of thoughts. At one point I remember thinking to myself, "I wonder, does anyone hear him?"

CHAPTER 17-"GOD THOUGHTS"

Thoughts about God were beginning to become noticeable to me. Probably because I hadn't had any for so long. The comment I had made to Joanne about only God being able to work out our marriage problems, now asking Bo to pray for us. It was strange for me to be thinking this way. I hadn't given a thought to anything spiritual in such a long time. It wasn't always that way. Growing up in a church, I had been taught about God, about Jesus. I remembered some of the thoughts and some of the times when I had prayed growing up. It seemed important to me to address the spiritual part of my life, even as a child, but I had never compiled enough experience to have formed a very definite view of who God was. I accepted what I was raised with, only because I was exposed to it, not because I had given it any thought and come to a conclusion about the matter. When I got to college, I stopped going to church entirely. After I broke up with my college girlfriend, I went through a tough time emotionally. I was distraught. That summer I took a job helping around the church I grew up in back in Sprngfield, working with the maintenance man on the property, mowing the lawns mostly. I remember spending time in the sanctuary on breaks, just sitting and sometimes praying for help with my lost love and little direction in my life. Things seemed to get better for me and I thought I had made a connection with God, whoever he was. I considered going back to school and studying to go into the ministry even. That didn't last though. I got into the long-hair, hippy lifestyle, which eventually led to me dropping out of school. Met Joanne, got married, two children later, moved to Alaska. Along the way I had experimented with everything from Hinduism to reincarnation. Nothing seemed to satisfy the questions I had and since I had been in Alaska, I put my quest to find truth aside. The drugs, some writing I had done, my whole lifestyle had really been part of what to me was a greater journey, an odyssey. I was a seeker, a thinker. I wanted to find meaning in life. I knew all the questions, but no answers. Part of going to Alaska was to get back to a natural place that I thought would make a difference. When that didn't happen, I just kind of stopped looking and resigned myself that maybe there was no concrete body of truth that we could know. We were all adrift on the existential sea of life, with little purpose and direction to give us meaning. If God had a way, it wasn't that well defined and he was keeping it hidden. One religion didn't seem much different to me than the next. It didn't seem to matter which one you chose. It depended it seemed on geography and culture, where you were born and how you were raised, as much as anything. I was born in America. I would be either Christian or Jewish. Japanese were Buddhists, Indians were Hindu, Arabs were Muslim.

Nothing of a personal nature to it at all, just head stuff, thoughts and philosophies, all pretty similar. They all talked about love and good works, living in harmony with ourselves and others but none of them seemed to have any power to enable us to live to that higher standard. I had always been dissatisfied with my life in that regard. My weaknesses and inabilities seemed always before me. If God was a force in our lives, he was so far out there, we could never know him, and he never seemed to affect us in a way that made our lives better or easier to endure. Maybe on rare occasions he would intervene, but not consistently. I never became atheistic, but I didn't know, at this stage in my life, if he was there for me or anyone else. I had long ago tired of trying to find out and he seemed to have long ago ceased from breaking into my circumstances in any significant way. If he was there, neither one of us was in touch with the other, or so it seemed to me.

Now here was Bo. His prayer was so sincere, as if he knew all about God. I wondered about that, but didn't pursue the thought. When he finished, I thanked him and went out to work. He had apparently forgiven me my transgression of the previous evening and I was relieved. As I started to work, I put the incident behind me, both the getting drunk and the prayer. I didn't give either anymore thought that day. Work done, I headed back again to the bar, but I was determined to keep the drinking within reasonable limits from then on.

CHAPTER 18-"WHAT NEXT ?"

I moved into the hotel room the following week. A bedroom, kitchen and living area. I wasn't prepared in any way to furnish or even fill up a room of any kind. Living out of my car for the last two weeks I was down to the bare necessities. I basically was using the bedroom and bathroom. That was it. I would go there from the bar to sleep. I ate out twice a day, breakfast and some dinner. It was a chance to mingle with people as well as take some sustenance. I couldn't see myself cooking in the room or having much on hand besides snacks. My culinary skills had never been developed beyond making camp food, bacon, eggs and hamburgers. I never liked to cook. As long as I could afford it, I would be a connoisseur of the fine restaurants of Haines. For me that meant a couple of breakfast diners and the restaurant by the bar. Maybe once in a while I'd go up to the hotel on the hill for a real dinner. I'd see as I went along.

Most of my time outside of work was still spent at the bar. I was becoming a steady customer, but really wasn't getting to know too many people yet. A lot of the clientele were passing through on their way to the ferry and points south. I would have a few drinks, play some pool, and usually head home about nine or ten. My time there each day amounted to probably a couple of hours. I was keeping the drinking under control and felt good about that.

I was calling home fairly regularly, to talk to Joanne and the girls. Michelle and Keri, I could tell, even over the phone, were not sure about what was going on. They sounded like they missed daddy, which was excruciating for me. I often had to hold back tears when talking to them. I kept telling them I'd be back in a while, but I knew that wasn't going to happen and I couldn't keep saying it.

Joanne was planning a trip back to Massachusetts in early September. Her mother was sending her the money to come. Just prior to our splitting up, her mom had visited us in Alaska for a couple of weeks. My relationship with her had always been on again, off again. Sometimes she liked me, sometimes it appeared she didn't. She had a lot of resentment toward the male gender in general and I was no exception. She had been hurt by her own divorce and never really recovered totally from it. I thought that she must have known about Joanne's plans to leave me and I wondered what her attitude toward that had been. We had a couple of good fights while she was with us. I half suspected she may have possibly encouraged the break-up. I don't know that for sure though.

Joanne and my conversations continued to be

uneventful. There was never any talk of me coming back home, which cut me to the core, but I was managing not to bring it up or appear to be begging. I wondered if she was going out, if there was another man. The thought of that would drive me crazy. I tried to avoid falling into that pit. I asked her if she was coming back to Alaska one night before she left. She said, "Of course I am," but I had my doubts. She would be leaving in a week. All I could do then was wait and see.

One night, in the early evening, I was sitting in the bar by the pool table. It was still light out, but the colors were starting to deepen as they do at the end of a sunny day, signaling the coming of the night. The wooden bar and tables and chairs had a deep, almost rich hue added to their natural color and there was a golden glow in the atmosphere that seemed to stream through the windows as if the sun wanted to leave us with a pleasant memory of the day and its light.

I had been drinking pretty steadily from about six o'clock. It was close to seven thirty now. I was in a peaceful, serene, almost good mood, but the melancholy that had been part of me for what seemed like such a long time now was still there at the corners of my mind, always intruding on any other thoughts and feelings I might have. I began again thinking about my circumstance, languishing in it was more the word. I watched the pretty blond waitress passing through the bar and restaurant, tending to her tasks. I had made no approaches to her since being here, though without a doubt, she was the most attractive female I had seen in this town. I wondered if she had noticed me in my comings and goings. We hadn't even exchanged greetings that I could remember.

Some of the locals were sitting up at the bar, drinking and laughing and carrying on as if they didn't have a care in the world. You knew better though. All you had to do was look into their eyes. Sometimes you saw tombstones there. Bars have a sad kind of energy and draw to their steady customers. There's a sharing of life amongst its members, a laugh here and there, a relationship, but in the end, much of it a sharing of the misery and heartbreak that most people seemed to want to drown in a drink and some small talk with a friend.

I began to think of my prospects for the future. The free and single life was deflating in my mind like a balloon with a slow leak. I hadn't enjoyed it in the least up until now and its continuance I knew would pull me into an ever-deepening depression. I thought, "Maybe I could start another relationship, get married again, have another family." Even that thought I realized was an admission to the fact that my present marriage seemed, for all intents and purposes to be irreconcilable. I was beginning to reluctantly accept that. It certainly seemed that way tonight. The thought of starting over again with someone new was like looking up at Mt. McKinley's north face. It was an unscalable height. I couldn't conceive of going through it again. You put everything into a marriage and family. It seemed that I had only been given the capacity to make that effort once in my life and it had failed. I looked again at the commiserating couples seated along the bar. Many of them I'm sure must have gone through gut-wrenching divorces. They wouldn't be here if they had a happy home to go to. I didn't want to become like that. Life had to offer more, but the thought crossed my mind and seemed to rivet me in my chair, the thought and the question, "Was there anything else? Was this going to be my future, my lot in life, all I had to look forward too? A beer, a game of pool, an empty, drab hotel room? Passing fancies and relationships that would only touch me on the surface? A little happiness mixed with much sorrow?" I couldn't stop thinking along this vein. I was frozen in it and haunted by it. There seemed to be a finality of resignation to it. It was like a whirlpool that wanted to suck me in, like the ocean pulls down a sinking ship. The pretty blond passed by again like a wisp of wind. Could I hope for anything more? It was too soon to give up completely, but I felt stifled, as if someone or something had a choke-hold on my soul. I had a couple of more beers and headed across the street for the night. These thoughts were too depressing and I wanted to shut them off in the bowels of sleep.

CHAPTER 19-"THE TERWILLIGERS"

August had slipped into September. The weather was still surprisingly warm. I didn't know if this was an Indian summer or if there was that much difference in the temperature between here and Anchorage. Signs of winter I knew were already in the air back there, a noticeable chill in the night, the trees changing their colors quickly, the bears roaming the mountain slopes, filling up on wild berries that seemed to grow everywhere in the fall. Not so here though. The days were still long and sunny and warm well into the evening.

I had begun framing on three of the five houses. There were two ranches and three split-entries. A split-entry was a one and a half story house, a full story above and a daylight basement below. These basements were half in the ground, the windows could be seen at ground level from the outside, the remainder of the floor was below ground. The front door opened on the landing of a stairway that went up to the living area and down to the basement rooms. Hence the name "split-entry". They were a popular design in Alaska, both here and up in the mainland. I think I could have built them blindfolded, I had framed so many over the time I had been in Alaska.

Bo and Wendell and now, Wendell's son, a new addition to our crew, were finishing pouring the final two foundations. Except for me, this was an all-church crew. I guessed church-goers stuck together in and out of the building. The plan was to get off the ground before winter, frame the basements and main floors and deck them. We would work on the upper stories and roofs afterwards. I was still doing all the framing myself. Bo had not hired a helper for me yet. There was some talk about Wendell and his family leaving before the winter, but I didn't know the details.

Joanne was back in Massachusetts with Michelle and Keri. I had talked to her the day she arrived, but not since then. Saturday, the sixth of September, was our fifth anniversary and I was planning to call her then. I was still hopeful that some word I could say or some sentiment I could express would turn this whole thing around and the separation would be over like waking from a bad dream. I always seemed to think this way. I could remember back before Joanne, when I broke up with girlfriends, thinking that some look of love could rekindle the dying flames. I had listened to too many "fifties" love songs or watched too many soapy movies. Life wasn't like that, but I would call Saturday with that hope.

Bo's family came up for the week from Juneau. They arrived on Tuesday. His wife was a woman of strong character. That was immediately apparent when you met her. She ran a tight ship in that little trailer. She knew what was going on all the time with her kids and with Bo, and the trailer became a real home while she was there. Meals were regular, the inside got a cleaning it hadn't seen in some time and the outside even got a face lift, looking more tidy and organized. The atmosphere of the construction site was buoyed by this woman's presence on the scene. She had a thick Scandinavian accent like her husband, and her voice carried. You could hear her from almost anywhere on the street, barking orders to her kids, who towed the line unquestionably.

The children, an older girl and two younger boys, were nice kids. The daughter was twelve or thirteen, the boys seven and ten. It was bittersweet for me having them around. The boys were playing all day, on the site and in the woods behind the houses. They were noisy and fighting like normal siblings, and it reminded me of Michelle and Keri and their little squabbles. I missed them so. I would have given anything to arbitrate one of those fights now.

The Bos were a noticeably happy family. He and his wife showed affection to each other and the kids seemed secure, they knew the bounds and limits of their lives and seemed to accept them. I generally liked being around them. I felt more in my realm, though at times it thrust my thoughts homeward, which never failed to bring a twinge of pain inside. It made me anticipate Saturday all the more. Surely she would be in a sentimental mood on our anniversary.

The day finally came. I worked that morning until about noon. I figured to call Joanne just after twelve and catch her at supper time, five hours difference, back on the east coast. Bo knew I was going to make the call, and I think knew my expectations were high concerning it. He offered to let me call her from the trailer.

I changed out of my work clothes, cleaned up and showered, as if I was going to actually see her, and walked back from the hotel to make the call. The phone was in the living area of the trailer. Bo and his family were in the kitchen eating lunch. I think they all knew I was calling Joanne. I guess he had filled his wife in on my situation. They seemed concerned for me.

I could hear the phone ringing. Joanne was at her brother's house. My sister-in-law answered and I said "hello" and talked to her for a minute. The girls weren't in the house, they were outside playing with their cousins. I asked for Joanne.

"Hi, how are you?"

"Okay", she replied

"You having a good time back there?" "Yeah" was all.

"You know what today is?" "Yeah", again.

"Had any thoughts about us?"

"Carl, don't start this. We 're separated and that's the way it going to stay."

Those words were like a knife in my heart. She was uncharacteristically cold, not the slightest sound of any warmth in her voice.

"I thought today being our anniversary, you might have a change of heart, thinking back." My voice trailed off through the five thousand miles of wires. I felt farther than even that from her at that moment.

"No Carl, I'm not thinking that way."

"Do you miss me at all?" I was desperate for anything.

"Stop Carl."

"Okay," I said dejectedly, "tell the girls I said 'hi' and I miss them. I love you. Good-bye."

"Good-bye."

I hung up the phone and sat by it for a moment stunned. My dreams of any warm feelings had crashed like a house of cards. There was silence in the trailer. The Bos seemed to sense what was happening with me. You could have heard a pin drop and I'm sure they heard me when I began to cry. There was a flood of tears inside me waiting to get out, they'd been waiting since I left Anchorage. I took a deep breath and sighed, loud enough that it was heard in the other room. I fought back the tears again, got up, walked toward the door of the trailer and sort of leaned on the counter going into the kitchen. The whole family looked up at me with a real concern, even the kids. I didn't have to explain what had happened.

"Is the church open?" I asked. "I'd like to go up there and sit for a while."

"Yes, I'm sure it is Carl," Bo replied. "Do you want me to call Wendell and have him meet you?"

"No, I just want to go up there and sit for a while. I'll be okay. See you later."

"You know how to get there?"

"Yeah, I think so. I'll find it."

I left the trailer and headed for my car. I was numb. What kept me in motion I don't know. As I drove toward the church, I thought to myself, "What am I doing? I'm in Alaska. I could go in almost any direction and be in the middle of nowhere in a few minutes. What am I doing going to a church?"

I thought about turning back, but I kept going. My mind went back to when I was a kid and liked to sit in the sanctuary of the church I grew up in. It was quiet and peaceful and God was supposed to hang around there. Maybe it was the memory of that summer sitting in that same place again, through a tough time, and feeling like I'd made a connection with the

Almighty. I felt comfortable in the quiet there. I always had. But I hadn't been in a church for so long. That night in Haines Junction, when I slept on the old wooden pews of that tiny Yukon church was the first time in probably two, maybe three years.

I pulled up in front of the building, parked the car and headed for the main door. It opened and Wendell came out. Bo must have called him and told him I was coming. I really didn't want to talk to anyone, but I was here now and felt sort of trapped. I knew he meant well, just wanted to help. I didn't say anything about it and we went inside together.

I was so distraught, I didn't really notice anything about what the church looked like. It seemed rather dim inside. I don't know why, it was mid-afternoon. I sat down in a pew. Wendell sat beside me. This was a kind man. I felt nothing but compassion coming from him. He didn't seem to have any agenda, he was just there to help.

"I just talked to my wife back in Massachusetts. You know we're separated. That's where we're originally from. She's back there visiting family. Today is our five-year anniversary. I thought it might mean something to her, that she might reconsider what's happening. She was cold as ice. It just hurts, it hurts bad. I never wanted this, I never wanted any of it. I love her, I love my kids. I want to be with them, not here."

A lot of information to open a conversation with.

The tears just started coming. Like a river, they kept coming. They'd been waiting. From some deep well within me they came. I sobbed, even though Wendell was there. It didn't matter anymore. They had to come sometime. My insides had to be washed. It's as if the tears were doing that for me, washing out the deposits of hurt and pain that had been collecting since all this began.

Wendell put an arm around my shoulder.

After a few minutes, I don't even know how long, I felt the flood begin to subside. "Everything seemed okay with us. I never saw this coming. I don't know what to do now."

"Carl, you don't have to go through this alone. There's someone who wants to help. He knows what you're going through. It's Jesus. He's here for you if you want His help."

I didn't know what to say to this. I was silent, just listening.

"I want to pray with you Carl. I want to ask Jesus to show you that He's here. I want to pray for you and Joanne, your marriage. Will that be okay?"

"Yeah, sure, I guess so."

"Jesus, show Carl who You are. Show him that you care about all this and that You can help him."

He went on. I lost touch with the words. I

started thinking about Bo's prayer a week ago and now Wendell's. I remember how I questioned when Bo prayed if anyone was listening. I had my head in my hands again, like with Bo, as Wendell was praying now. My thoughts had changed now. I remember distinctly thinking to myself, "I hope someone hears this. I hope." I had come a step from where I had been, a step from skepticism to hope. I wanted God or Jesus or someone to be there.

Wendell finished his prayer. He had a Bible with him. He handed it to me. "Carl, take this home with you. Just read it at night or in the morning, whenever. Start with the book of John. Would you do that?"

"Yeah, I guess it wouldn't hurt anything." This man was so gracious and unassuming. I might never open the book, but I couldn't say "no" to him. I took the Bible from him.

"Come on next door, I want you to meet my family."

We got up from the pew, left the main church building and walked behind it to the parsonage where Wendell lived. I remembered, as I walked across the grass that afternoon, this was the house I drove by the night I was drinking with the Canadians. I remembered the warm glow of the light coming from the windows, a light that almost invited you inside. Now here I was at the threshold.

Wendell's family greeted me like I was a long-lost son coming home. It's like I knew them all my life.

They seemed so glad to see me, a total stranger. His wife was a pretty lady, bubbly, full of life. His son and his wife were there. I had met him on the job briefly. They greeted me with open arms. They were newlyweds, married just four months. Wendell had a younger daughter too. She was fifteen.

We just started talking. They asked me where I was from. When I told them New England, they all were thrilled. "Oh. we want to go there someday and see Boston and Cape Cod and Maine."

"Yeah, they're all beautiful. Been to all those places. Lived in Boston for two years. Went to school there. Maine's as much Alaska as any place you'll see in the East. There's wilderness areas and moose there."

The small talk continued the rest of the afternoon. They showed such a genuine interest in me, it kind of took me back. They were so willing to tell me about themselves too. Wendell's wife brought out some sandwiches and I ate with them. His son and daughter-in-law showed me their wedding pictures. They were all getting ready to leave Haines. Wendell was going to Seattle to be the minister in a church down there. They had been here for four years and didn't really want to leave, but a retired missionary who had been in Africa for many years was coming up to take over this church. Apparently the organization they were ministers with felt it was the best arrangement for Wendell and the older missionary. The son and daughter-in-law were going to go to school down there to become missionaries.

We talked on through the rest of the afternoon. They didn't want me to leave. They invited me for supper, but I told them I kind of wanted to get back to the hotel and go to bed early. I was tired. I thanked them for their hospitality, took the Bible Wendell had given me, and headed back down the hill to the hotel.

I couldn't get over how outgoing this family was. I had not met people ever before like this in Alaska. They were so unreserved in their giving to me. They had lifted the load I was carrying from off my shoulders and bore it with me for a time. I remembered going up that hill so heavy with cares. I really felt better now, thanks to this family's willingness to just take me into their lives for that afternoon. I put the Bible on the nightstand by the bed and thought, "Maybe I will read it." I found the book of John and started that night. I was soon sound asleep, the end of a long day.

CHAPTER 20-"AGONY"

Another week went by. Nothing had really changed much. My routine was the same, with the exception that I was reading the Bible a little each morning before work and usually at night before I fell asleep. I didn't understand much of what I read. It all seemed kind of vague. It was definitely about Jesus, I knew that much. I would see Wendell and Bo each day at work. They never really said anything more to me about that Saturday, but I knew they were still concerned for me. They had a caring attitude all the time toward me.

The work was progressing on the houses. I had the basements pretty much framed on the splits by the second week of September and had completed the floors on the ranches. Summer was making its last stand, the days were getting a little shorter, the nights a little colder. The flow of tourists through the town had almost ceased. All I'd see at the bar and restaurants these days were the locals.

Happily, Joanne had returned from Massachusetts, but nothing had changed in our situation. I was still calling on occasion, mostly talking to Michelle and Keri. Joanne and I weren't saying much beyond formalities since that disastrous anniversary conversation. I was sending her money, now that paychecks were starting to come in again.

The blond waitress was suddenly gone. I guessed that maybe she was back in school somewhere in the "lower forty-eight". I felt like a bear preparing for hibernation. The town seemed to be drawing in on itself, moving slower, more determinedly with winter coming on. Alaskan winters, I had found, were something to be endured. Their defining characteristic is their length. They are long, late September to sometimes early June. Not as severe as I had envisioned when I first came here, but long. My first winter in Anchorage was a challenge. I wanted to see if I could make it through. Working outside made it even more of a personal test. After two or three had gone by though the thrill was gone. Now they were just long and you didn't want to think about how long in September. I didn't know what to expect in Southeastern. Winters here were an unknown to me. I could tell already it would be warmer and that I might see more rain than snow. I thought this might be more like Seattle than Anchorage.

Bo had mentioned possibly letting me stay in a trailer he had on another lot a short ways up the street from where he was building. Said he wouldn't charge me anything to stay there, I could watch it for him. Thought he could save me some money since I was supporting my family away from here. It was a nice gesture, but being fiercely prideful and independent,

I thought I would make my own way at the hotel. Again, I was struck by how out of character this kind of generosity was to me in construction circles. I had never met a contractor like him, especially not in Anchorage. Back there we were all so self-serving, like a bunch of gunslingers from the old West, everyone looked out for himself and you didn't trust anybody. I remember times getting paid with hundred-dollar bills in the front seats of pick-up trucks by men with guns laid on the seats beside them or a fist-fight I had had one time at the home of an employer who didn't pay me. I couldn't imagine Bo ever doing anything like that. It took me some time to let my guard down with him, but 1 eventually did. I enjoyed working for him and wanted to do a good job. Even though I took less in wages, my expenses were fairly low and what I was making seemed to be enough. If I eventually moved to his trailer, it would be even better, so financially, at least for now, my mind was at ease, and I continued my routine of work and drink and sleep. Still no pot to be had, but I didn't seem to miss it too much. This was as long as I had gone without any in the six years I had been smoking it.

I had been in the hotel about two weeks now. It was a Wednesday evening. I had left the bar early and lay in my bed reading the Bible in John, the book Wendell had suggested. The English was so stiff and formal, I was having a hard time understanding what I was reading, and my eyes were getting heavy as I continued. Soon I fell asleep, with the book in my lap and the light by my bed still on.

I woke at first light the next day. Some of the windows in the hotel had no curtains or shades, so enough light shone into the room to wake me early, even though I had forgotten to set an alarm. I noticed the light by the bed was still on and 1 had rolled over on the Bible while I slept. I got up and took a quick shower, shaved and dressed. I still had some time before I needed to get on to work. I didn't think I'd eat anything this morning, I'd wait 'till noon and get a hamburger at the restaurant at the end of the street then.

I straightened up my bed and in moving the Bible decided I would read a few minutes before heading out. I started where I remembered leaving off the night before, determined in my mind to try and make some sense of what I was reading.

All I knew is that this was the story of Jesus' life or at least excerpts from it chosen by the author. John didn't talk about the birth of Jesus. I noticed that. I wondered why it wasn't there, not realizing at the time it was in another of the books. Some of the passages seemed vaguely familiar, probably I had heard them read or spoken in church when I was growing up. I remembered back to when I was a little boy just learning to read. My mom and dad had a big Bible with all kinds of pictures in it, pictures that had that Michelangelo look of the Sistine ceiling. God was an old man with long, flowing white hair. I remember having the desire to read the whole book back then, laying on the floor of our living room, reading and looking at those pictures. I could remember some of them, one of Abraham, with a beard that looked like it went down to his knees, and one of a scene with Jacob and Joseph and a bunch of other people, one of Joseph and his fancy coat, asleep and dreaming about some stalks of wheat. They were lithographs, black and white. It amazed me that I could remember them after all these years. They had left an impression. I don't remember anything beyond Joseph except a vague memory of another picture, of Moses holding the Ten Commandments, but I don't remember reading anything about him. I lost interest after Genesis. Maybe that's when we got our first TV.

Genesis was full of stories though and I remembered particularly the one about Jacob and Joseph reuniting after Jacob had thought Joseph was dead. What a story, it moved me even as a boy. John was telling a story too, about Jesus, but I couldn't connect the events very well and had no idea where it was going. I got frustrated again and lay the book down on my nightstand. I thought I would just go ahead and walk to work since I had some extra time.

I went into the bathroom, brushed my hair, checked out my beard, which covered my face pretty well by now. I liked its look, not too long, kind of scruffy and full. Gave me what I thought was that tough, slightly detached look of a wandering troubadour or some kind of folk-hero. I wanted that sort of image. I guess

I saw myself that way when I went through my writing period back in Massachusetts. I had a sort of charisma I thought with my friends. Being a writer, I think they thought I had answers of some sort to life's questions. I knew better, which is why I eventually gave it up. I still held on to that image though and had always tried to see myself that way during that period of my life. What a misrepresentation of the facts of who I was.

I brushed my teeth and rinsed my mouth. The tap water was cold and refreshing. I headed back to the bedroom for my wallet and was about to leave. I sat down on the bed for a moment. It's funny how thoughts can change so suddenly, and when thoughts change and take you somewhere else with them, emotions follow at their heels like a puppy-dog that follows its mother everywhere she goes and anywhere she leads him. I was not thinking about Joanne, but she came to my mind just for a moment. A picture of her face formed clearly, almost as if she was there. I hadn't missed her like this since I left and with my whole insides I cried out with a plaintive sort of cry. I fell off the bed and onto the floor in a heap and began to beat the floorboards with my elbows and hands in a kind of twisted agony. I felt as if I was rolled up in a fetal position and continued to cry out with a pain that came from deep within. I couldn't tell at first if I was shedding any tears, it was a cry of pain from some recess of my soul, a cry for her, a cry for something that would make reason of what had happened to us.

I half-struggled to a kneeling position when my thoughts suddenly shifted to God. Somehow, I could see myself in a heap on this bare floor and a picture of my condition came clearly to me.

CHAPTER 21-"FLASHBACK"

A number of years earlier, while still in Massachusetts, during my quest for understanding life, I was thinking about joining a semi-religious commune, tucked away in the hills of Western Massachusetts. I had visited it with some friends and Joanne the previous weekend and couldn't get my mind off the place since we had returned home. I had hitchhiked up there three days later to take another look around, with the thought already in my mind that I might want to live there.

Joanne had put up with a lot from me. I had basically left working steadily at that time and we were surviving meagerly on unemployment, welfare and odd-jobs. I was throwing myself completely into my writing and somehow justified what I was doing as some sort of "cause-celebre" in my mind.

I had tried Eastern religions, read some of the Koran, followed a Hindu guru, chanted with Hare Krishna's, read Edgar Cayce, consulted with spiritists, dropped acid, you name it. The commune was a mix of all these paths it seemed, with some consideration of Jesus and the apostles thrown in, probably due to the influence of the member's upbringings in

Christian churches. The leader of this place believed he was the reincarnation of Peter the apostle. He was supposed to be able to see auras and when I met him, he acted as if I was someone special, or so I imagined. I never minded people feeling this way toward me. I often thought more of myself than I should have in those days. I almost believed for a time that I did have something to say. I had even envisioned myself one time being an eyewitness at the death of Jesus, so I probably thought I already knew Michael and he recognized me from the past, the distant past of some other Edgar Cayce life. Crazy stuff.

When I left home to go back there at the time, I could tell Joanne was not happy. She was not impressed at all with the place or with the people there. If I had come home wanting to take them there with me, I probably would have been told, "adios," and rightfully so.

I got to the commune in the early afternoon and was told I could stay in one of the large dormitories that night. I could take my meals with the "family" too. There were others there in the visitor's quarters, which were rows of bunk-beds in what looked like an Army barracks. I remembered a mother and her daughter and a pretty young girl with a child who were there that week too, for the same reason I was, to check the place out.

I talked with some of the residents of the commune that afternoon. These people were pretty far out there and idolized the self-proclaimed prophet/leader of the group, Michael. He was the guy who thought he was Peter. I ate in the dining area with the families. I looked for Michael but didn't see him that night. It was dark when I had finished eating and I was having a cup of tea, still in the dining hall, when a man, who looked to be older than me, maybe mid-thirties, took a seat next to me at the table I was sitting at.

We said hello and began talking. He asked me why I was there. I told him. We talked for a long time at the table. I felt I could be open with this guy and began to share my feelings about the world's religions. Being a pilgrim in search of truth and a writer, I could certainly speak with authority on the universality of religious thought, how all religions were basically similar and relied on the same fundamental truths of love and brotherhood, and charity etc. I was sure he would be impressed by my knowledge of these things. I say that with a note of sarcasm today.

Much to my surprise, he wasn't. I thought we would be in agreement on everything. Most of the other people I had talked to there, if you spun a goofy enough existential web, they would affirm their agreement with an all-inclusive, "yeah man, far out" reply. This man was different. He seemed to be arguing with me, in a nice way, at every point. We left the dining room and walked outside, embroiled still in our deep discussion. We wandered around the grounds of the commune for what seemed like most of the night. This man raised disturbing questions in my thinking. Somehow, he was saying that "no, religions weren't all alike", that there was someone or something that was different and stood out from the rest, though honestly, at that time, I didn't know who or what that was, and I can't remember any revelation from him concerning that. He was persistent and determined and I remember late that night leaving him and saying I would probably see him in the morning. I couldn't find out if he was staying in the dorm where I was. He didn't come in with me, so I don't know if he stayed there or someplace else. This was the only visitors' dorm I knew of at the commune. I never saw him again after. He simply left, walking up the road slowly, hands tucked in the pockets of his jeans, head slightly bowed, shoulders slumped forward, away from the place, like a hobo from a Woody Guthrie song, fading into the night. I had looked for him the following day, but he was mysteriously gone. He had left his mark on my thinking though. Suddenly I could see as clear as crystal the contradictions of the commune, the real sense of emptiness and desperation in its people, the idol-worship toward Michael and the real danger that that could lead to. This was a last stand for many of these people. They had grown hopelessly disenchanted with everything in life and wanted this place to work for them. This man I had met I knew had an influence in this train of thought. I felt a strength and an ability to see clearly into my present circumstance. It was almost like that night before Joanne and I got married when I had such a clear insight into what was needed in our relationship. I felt that same kind of confidence the next day, even if I didn't understand where these feelings emanated from, and I didn't.

I spent the morning at the commune. I had a made the decision to leave right away, knowing somehow that it was the right thing to do. I knew Joanne would be relieved to hear this when I got home.

Before I left I spent some time with the mother and daughter who were there, with whom I had had some short conversations during the previous day. The mother told me that she never wanted to move there, she had only come because her daughter did and she was afraid for her. They were leaving too and I told her I thought they had made the right decision, that this place really didn't have any answers. I packed the few belongings I had in the knapsack I had brought and headed down the stairs of the dorm on my way back home.

The pretty blond girl was just outside the door, standing with her baby and walking around slowly, I think trying to put her child to sleep. We had also talked and were friendly toward each other. I went to her to say "good-bye". A strong urge to warn her welled up inside me as I approached her.

"I'm going home to my family. This isn't the place I thought it was. I think there's danger here. Take your little girl and go home. Don't stay!"

She looked at me and smiled and I saw what appeared to be agreement in her eyes.

"Thanks, Carl. I am. God be with you."

"Yeah," I replied, "remember now, you take your baby and leave, the sooner the better. Good-bye."

I headed back down the road toward home. The day was a beautiful sunny one and the shade of the mountain trees blocked out the direct rays of the midday sun. There was a coolness in the shade as I walked out of the mountains, toward the main highway and home, riding my thumb. I felt liberated from a lot of confusion somehow that had been so much a part of me up to that day. I felt that strength and confidence again coming from a source, whether in me or out of me I didn't know, that seemed to carry the day. That man last night had something to do with it all, but I could remember little of what he said now and his physical features were fading fast in my memory, even though it was just a short time ago we had talked.

I made a determination that day on the way home that from then on I was going to quit reading about other people's opinions about life and from my own experience determine my own truth. No more Bible, Jesus, Koran, Mohammed, Kahil Gibran, Meher Baba, the Beatles, Bob Dylan, Neil Young, James Taylor. I would find my own way, break my own paths, find truth that would work for me in my life.

CHAPTER 22-"CRYING
OUT TO GOD"

Two years later now, kneeling on that floor in the hotel room in Haines, some of those memories came back to me as I moaned and groaned over my condition. My search for my truth, my determination to be my own trailblazer and find my own way had brought me from that day in Massachusetts to Alaska, to cynicism, and now to this. I had almost unconsciously left off even trying to find answers anymore. The memories that passed through my mind today were the first thoughts I had had on the subject in I couldn't remember how long. My quest had been lost somewhere along the way. I had over time given up. I realized that today. Now here I was, on my knees in pain, my wife and family eight hundred miles away, nothing to show for the effort but failed relationships and the clothes on my back, a worn tee-shirt, a pair of jeans, work boots, a few tools in my car. That was it. My noble endeavor had brought me to a heap on the floor of life.

Clasping my hands together and looking up toward the ceiling. I cried, "God, if you're there I have to know. I need you. I need to know if I'm alone in this or not. Show me if you're there. Please!"

My prayer life had come a long way in the last two weeks. From skepticism to hope to actually praying myself. I hoped that those words had wings. Wings to take them up, past the ceiling and roof, beyond the clouds and sky to the place where God was, if there was such a place.

Nothing happened at that moment, no voice from heaven or choir of angels spoke or sang. I felt better though and the pain and tears were for the moment gone. I got up and went to work, thinking of nothing in particular, kind of numbed by the catharsis of emotion I had just been through.

CHAPTER 23-"THE MOMENT"

The physical nature of the work I did helped me almost forget about the entire incident. I guess I figured the tears were just more reaction to Joanne's and my breakup. Crying from time to time had become almost a normality, a therapy for dealing with the hurt inside. By mid-morning I had forgotten it and went to the restaurant at noon to eat.

I appreciated the kind of work I had chosen for a trade. Framing had periods of mental activity, laying out and planning the building of the floor, the walls, the roof, followed by the physical activity of doing the tasks. Your mind could wander during the physical times, but not too far. Using saws and walking joists and top plates and rafters required that you kept your wits about you. Daydreaming was out and to some degree dangerous.

Thoughts would come and go though on occasion. That was what happened that afternoon. A thought came to me from God, from wherever he was, away from that house I was working on, yet there at the same time.

It was around two in the afternoon. I was framing the floor on one of the single-story ranches, blocking a row of joists, bent over just pounding nails. The day had been bright and sunny and warm. My mind was on my work, nothing else. A single thought, not an audible voice, but in some sense it was as if someone was speaking into my mind, into the depths of my soul, into my heart. "I'm here," that was it.

Something in me had distinctly heard it. I stopped for a moment and looked around, as if I expected Him to walk out from the woods at the edge of the lot and join me. I had heard Him. There was an impression of the fact of His being there that had come from a place definitely outside of me. I suddenly knew it, nothing within me doubted that. It's like something I knew as sure as I knew I was alive, or that the sky was blue and the sun was a yellow orb shining in it. I knew that I knew that there was a God out there and that He knew that I was here and that I was hurting and that I had cried out to Him that morning. I felt better, more than better. It's as if something was lifted off of me that I'd been carrying for a long, long time, a weight of circumstance, the burden of not knowing the fact of His existence. This revelation seemed to be changing me from moment to moment.

There was a sense of relief in my soul, He was there, I wasn't alone anymore. The relief was tangible, I could feel it. It began to have an effect physically on me. I had never understood or experienced in my life a sense of joy. That's the only way I can describe the feelings that seemed to be coursing through my being in greater and greater waves of emotion. I took off

Carl Gove

my nail bags and stood on the floor for a moment, taking it all in. It exhilarated me, it moved me. I walked off the foundation and walked around the lot, shaking my head, almost in disbelief, but this was not a thought that had come from me and I would never shake it. I didn't want to shake it. That joy I felt was at that moment all consuming. Everything would be all right, He was there, I was not alone anymore.

I jumped into the air, standing where I was on the lot. I wanted to jump some more. I wanted to shout. I took off down the street toward where I knew Bo and Wendell were working. I had no consciousness of anyone seeing me running like this, but if a stranger did, I didn't really care what they thought. This was real. I was running almost full speed when I approached Bo and Wendell. They looked up and saw me bounding towards them and stopped what they were doing. They looked a bit perplexed, not knowing if something was wrong.

From a distance I began shouting to them, "I'm saved, I'm saved! God is real!"

They looked at me in amazement, who knows what they were thinking. I got to where they were standing, stopped and exclaimed again, not shouting this time, they were standing right there. "I must be saved. God just spoke to me, told me He's here for me. I know I'm not alone now in this!"

I think one of them responded to me, "That's great Carl, I'm happy for you." I don't know if it was Bo or

Wendell who said it, I think Wendell. I remember that big grin that Bo was always ready with, lighting up his face.

I took off running again back toward the house, running a ways and jumping into the air as I went. This had to be joy, I had no other word to describe the feeling. I was changed by that one thought in that one moment. Everything was different now. I knew it. He was there, I was not alone anymore.

CHAPTER 24-"CHANGES"

After that day, things really became different. My circumstances had not changed externally, but internally was another story. God's presence became a part of my life. I knew He was with me all the time. I wondered if He had time for anyone else, He seemed to be around me constantly. I appreciated the attention. I thought about Him, I talked to Him. I continued reading the Bible, now with a renewed enthusiasm, but it still didn't make a lot of sense. There was a hope though in my life that wasn't there before. I was even hopeful about the future, about Joanne and myself.

I started to go to church with Bo, Sunday mornings and nights and a Bible study and prayer time on Wednesday nights. The people in the church were just nice people. They said they had been praying for me for a number of weeks and my being there was an answer to those prayers. So I was somewhat of a celebrity it seemed. They were very kind to me, treated me like parents do their kids.

About the time I had my revelation, as I called it, Wendell and his family were ready to leave for Seattle. They were all so happy about what had happened with me. I was sorry to see them leave, a truly warm group of people.

The new minister had arrived from where I don't know. He was a retired missionary, spent a good deal of his life somewhere in Africa. His name was Don and he was with his wife Wilma. They had two daughters, but they were grown and on their own. They moved into the parsonage that adjoined the church, where Wendell's family had just vacated

This man reminded me of my own father, a kind and gentle and humble soul. He spoke softly, his voice wavering a bit with his age. As a preacher, he was not very dynamic, in fact he almost would put me to sleep. But he had a warm, kind character that drew you in. He was a shepherd to his flock, caring for them. Rumor had it that he would pray individually every day for each member of the church. He took an immediate interest in my situation and took time whenever I saw him to ask about how things were. Though his sermons were dull I wanted to be in the church and kept attending regularly with Bo. I looked forward to being there, sensing that this connection I had made with God was staying with me and even growing.

The church had about fifty members, mostly older, straight, very conservative people. I was a bit of an oddity in appearance, with my beard and scraggly hair and clothes, but they accepted me. To them I was like a newborn, they wanted to see me keep growing in this relationship with God.

There were a few young families in the congregation and I began to develop a close friendship with one of them almost from the start of attending. His name was Terry, his wife's name, Linnus. They had a year-old daughter and were long-hair types like me, though Terry's hair and beard were much more groomed than mine. We had things in common and they started asking me over for dinner during the week, at least once or twice. I felt as though I could come and go at their house and started visiting them quite a bit after work and on weekends. Linnus' cooking was great and a welcome change. I had been eating restaurant food for almost a month.

Terry was a reformed drug addict. At one time he was pretty bad and for a period he withdrew into a deep shell that his wife and family feared he would never come out of. He barely communicated with anybody and was detached from people who tried to talk to him. There was some thought of committing him to an institution and he was so far gone he didn't seem to care and was putting up no resistance to his family's plans. He was not functioning at all and would just spend hours sitting in a trancelike state. His wife didn't know what to do, though she had had her problems too with drugs.

I don't know all the details, but somehow they had hooked up with a church much like the one we were attending, though not here in Haines, and "found Jesus". Terry's recovery was dramatic. He came out of himself and started functioning again, without the drugs. He just stopped. Linnus followed. They had left wherever they were when all this happened and came up here to Alaska. Terry worked in the local sawmill I had passed on my way into town from Canada. The baby was born here and Linnus stayed home with her.

People from the church started asking me over to dinner almost regularly. I was rarely having to eat out anymore. When I wasn't at Terry and Linnus' I was at someone else's place. I got to know almost everybody within a couple of weeks. They were the nicest group of people I had ever met in Alaska. Being around them kind of kept my spirits up, that and the sense of God being in it all.

I just stopped going to the bar. Between the church services and eating out and spending time at Terry's, I rarely had a night free and stopped going there with hardly a thought about the change. Bo had offered again to let me stay in the trailer on the property and I moved my few belongings from the hotel one Saturday and took up my new residence there.

It was an old trailer, needing paint. The toilet didn't work, but the sink and shower did. The lights and the refrigerator were turned on, so even without the toilet, it was livable. The bedroom in the back was where I kept everything and spent most of my time. I never even found out if the stove was on. My opportunity to develop my culinary skills was passing me by. I had extra money now, since I moved out of the hotel, and I could afford to eat out pretty much whenever I wanted, though with all the home cooking I was getting from the church members, I didn't even do that very much. I would eat breakfast or lunch at one of the local restaurants when I was hungry and once in a while Bo and I would go out to eat dinner at the seafood restaurant adjacent to the bar. That was all the place saw of me anymore. I hadn't had a drink since my experience on the job and still no pot. Honestly, I wasn't even thinking about it.

I began to read my Bible with a passion. I wanted to know all about this God and from what I learned at church, the Bible was His book. Every morning I would read some from the Old and New Testaments and I got a devotion tract from the church and began to read it each day. I tried to pray to Him too, though at times I didn't know what to say. What do you talk about with God? A lot of times my mind would be blank and I found myself developing a pattern of asking for my wife to have an experience like mine. I wrote to her about it, telling her that I'd found what we were all looking for all these years as long-hairs. I got no response back from her right away. Over time I began to have a sense that if what happened to me could happen to her, our marriage could be saved. God would be the key. I remembered back to those words I spoke to her before I left, "I guess I'll have to pray to God, he's the only one who can put this back together again." I didn't know at the time what I was *saying, now the truth of that statement seemed so real.*

I don't remember how this got started, but I got a key to the church from the pastor and would drive up there each morning before work and spend some time in the sanctuary praying for Joanne. I'd just ask God to show Himself to her, like He had to me. It was becoming a habit. The church was close enough that I would even drive up there during lunch breaks for a few moments, not eating, maybe stopping on the way back at the restaurant for an ice cream, which I'd eat in the car as I drove. My life was becoming consumed with this fresh relationship with a God who was suddenly alive and well and near to me. My thoughts often centered on Him, on my life in relationship to all I was reading and hearing about from the Bible and the sermons at church. Conversations around the dinner tables of the members, especially Terry and Linnus, were having their effect too. I was changing it seemed daily and caught up in it all The trips to the church gave me time to reflect on it all.

CHAPTER 25-"JESUS ???"

We had an Indian summer that year in Alaska. Warm temperatures lingered into mid-September, and the winter rains I had heard so much about here were nowhere in sight. The days were bright and sunny and balmy and I was still wearing only a tee-shirt and jeans to work. Bo had added an additional laborer to the crew since Wendell had left. His name was Bob and he pretty much worked with me, hauling studs and lumber for whatever I was doing.

He was a long-hair, on his way back to the states. He figured on working for Bo for a few weeks to make enough money to book passage on the ferry to Seattle and have some traveling change when he got there. A quiet guy, short and stout, with medium length mousy-brown hair and a full beard, I could tell he was a pot-head. He talked kind of slow, his tone almost detached, his words sometimes slurred. I wondered if he had any pot with him once, but I never pursued it further. I had no desire to get high. I felt as though I had been on a high for weeks with God.

Bob picked up soon that Bo and I were churchgoers. It seemed funny to me to be on the other side of the fence from where I was just a few weeks before.

Because of my conversion, as Bo referred to it, he felt as though he was on a roll getting people "saved" and was soon inviting Bob to every service we went to. He came on a couple of Sunday mornings, I think to be polite to his boss, but really wasn't interested.

Time passed and I started to pick up some of the Christian "lingo" I was hearing more and more at church and Bible studies and prayer meetings. As far as I could understand I had been converted to Christ and "saved", though I wasn't sure yet from what. The Bible was "God's Word", which meant that He inspired the people who wrote it. I was a "born-again" Christian now. I knew that something had changed in me, so I didn't have much resistance to what I was hearing and pretty much accepted it without question.

I got baptized after one of the Sunday morning services. The whole church went over to one of the other churches in town after our morning service. They went there because they had a baptismal, which our church didn't have. It was a small tank of water that looked like a swimming pool, painted with that turquoise color that helped the water look cleaner than it maybe was. Everyone sat in the pews except Don and I. We stood at the front of the church on opposite sides of the baptismal. I had changed into a pair of shorts and a white tee-shirt and got into the water down a stairway from one side of the tank while Don entered from a stairway on the other. He asked me to say a few words about my "conversion".

"Well, I came to Haines in pretty bad shape as most of you know. My wife and I had just separated. Somehow I came to the realization that I needed God in my life, if there was a God out there to be known. I wasn't sure at first. I prayed He would show Himself to me and He did. It has changed the way I feel about everything. Maybe my wife will find this too and our marriage can be saved. I want to keep going in this, that's why I want to be baptized, to kind of put a seal on what's happened. I thank God for what He's done."

Don said a short prayer asking God to be with me. Then he placed me in front of where he was standing in the water, turned me sideways and said as he dunked me completely under the water, "Carl, I baptize you in the name of the Father, and the Son and the Holy Spirit. Amen!"

That was it, everyone applauded and I left the pool soaking wet. I didn't have any special feeling coming out of the water, but somehow it seemed like the right thing to do if my intent was to continue on with God. I wanted that, so I did it. I thought to myself, "This sure is a lot different from the way we baptized back home." We brought our kids to my childhood church when they were babies and a priest or minister sprinkled a little "holy" water on their heads. I wondered why they did it this way, dunking me under, but didn't know the answer.

I was learning about God it seemed, here a little, there a little, but there was an awful lot I felt I just *didn't understand. Terry, Linnus and I would talk about the Bible over dinners in their house. They mentioned "heaven", "hell", the "devil", "eternal life" in our conversations. I had gone to church all my young life and was surprised how little I really knew about any of these subjects. Were heaven and hell real? I thought the devil was a metaphor.*

The subject, or I should say person, they spoke of most was Jesus. They talked a lot about Jesus. Jesus this, Jesus that, but not using the name the way I had been used to hearing it in the past. It had a different connotation in a curse. The way they talked, it was as if they knew him familiarly. Sometimes you expected him to show up at the door to eat with us. It's like he was always right there for them, like God was for me. I kind of wished I could show up a little earlier or later, whatever the case and catch him for a word or two and maybe some questions. I felt like I knew God, and of course I knew who Jesus was historically, but I sure didn't have a sense of knowing him the way Terry and Linnus seemed to. I thought about that in passing one night as I walked back to my trailer, but couldn't figure out what was going on with it all and let the thoughts pass. I figured, "Hey, I know God, I've been baptized, I read the Bible, go to their church. I'm just like them."

Another night I was at another couple's house from the church for dinner, Charlie and Faith Pease. Charlie worked at the sawmill with Terry and Faith was a housewife. Terry, Linnus, the Peases and I were all about the same age, but whereas Terry, Linnus and I came from a "hippie" background, Charlie and Faith had been raised in church, met at a church function, dated, got married and had a baby and seemed to be living happily ever after. Church life seemed to be all they knew. They were another exceedingly nice couple. I thought to myself sitting at the table, "Man, they sure have lived a sheltered life. They don't know anything about 'what's happening' out in the world. The longer I was there that night, embraced by the warmth of their home, the more I wondered if they needed to know anymore than they did. What they had was working. They were together and happy, more than I could say for my family.

After dinner, Charlie told me how when he was a young boy, he asked Jesus to forgive him for his sins and to come into his heart. Even though he was raised in church, he felt like he still had to do that. It sounded a lot like what I had done that morning in the hotel with God, but Jesus was the central figure of his conversation, while God was in mine, and sin wasn't involved. I felt like God was personal, but Charlie had a name for Him. It seemed even more personal than what I had. I just didn't relate to Jesus in the same way he did. I thought about that often now, but never talked to anybody about it. As time went on though I could see that all of my church friends, young and old, talked about Jesus in the same way, and I didn't. That bothered me, but it was something I just didn't understand.

CHAPTER 26-"THE HOLY SPIRIT ???"

I had been talking to Joanne and the kids fairly regularly on the phone. I told her about meeting God and how it had changed me. She was very skeptical, probably thought it was a ploy to win her back. I'd had a lot of "revelations" in the past that didn't stick. I could understand why she questioned this one at this early stage.

Michelle was in preschool and Keri was home with Joanne. The girls were really wondering by this time why I wasn't at home. I don't know what Joanne had told them. I still just said I was away working out of town.

I had firmly established the habit of praying for Joanne daily. It was becoming a ritual. With my key to the church, I could use it anytime. I went there often. I loved the quiet of the place. It seemed a step away from the busyness of the world and a step closer to God. I would sit and just repeat over and over her name to Him. "God save her. God show her You're there. Save our marriage." Nothing fancy about this. I was just talking my heart out to Him.

Somehow I felt He was hearing me. I had a real

hope that what had happened to me would someday happen to her and we would get back together. I don't really know where it started or how it grew, but it was real and motivated me to keep going to the church and praying.

One night Terry came by work and asked me to come over after I got off for dinner. He wanted to talk to me about something. Around five o'clock I rolled up my saws and cords for the day, went by the trailer, cleaned up a little, and headed down to his house.

Linnus had made spaghetti and meat balls. It reminded me of home. Joanne was Italian and cooked great spaghetti. Sometimes everything seemed to remind me of her. She was never far from me, a thought away. We ate and were drinking coffee after the meal when Terry opened up the conversation. He gave me a book called "Prison to Praise", written by an author I certainly didn't know. I looked at it. It had a picture of a dove on the cover with wings extended, looking like it was descending over the remainder of the cover. I thought to myself, "Oh, oh, what's this? Is he going to get weird on me?"

He explained to me that the book was about something called in Christian circles, "the baptism of the Holy Spirit". I thought I had already been baptized, so what was this? He said that it was something different that God wanted to do in believers' lives. The book would tell me about it better than he could. I had alot of questions, but took the book and said I would look at it. That was all he said that night. He did tell me that a group of people from different churches in Haines who had this common experience of being "baptized in the Spirit" met on Friday nights for a Bible study and "fellowship", the Christian term for a "get together". He wanted me to come with them this Friday. Terry was my best friend right now, so not wanting to disappoint him I said I would. I'd be over that night to go.

I finished my coffee and told them I was heading home. Taking the book with me I drove back to my trailer and started reading it that night.

All I knew about the "Holy Spirit" was I remembered having read something about it in the book of John. Jesus had said it was "like the wind, no one knew from whence it came or whither it went" to put it in good old "King James English" from the Bible translation I had. I thought, "maybe I'll learn something", but I was a bit skeptical. The book was unpretentious, and I wondered if it could contain anything of great content or worthy of much thought.

The first two chapters were about a concept that was new to me, thanking God for everything, good and bad. As I was in a bad way with my family, this thought intrigued me and kind of got me interested. Apparently, there is a verse in the Bible that says "in everything give thanks, for this is the will of God". The author went on to hypothesize that even when we were going through difficult times, if we trusted God was with us and would work things for good in our lives, we could be thankful through the tough times and that would help us get through them quicker, or something to that effect. I thought that maybe if I started to thank God for the separation, He would end it sooner and Joanne and I would get back together. I was looking for a fix and maybe my relationship with God would provide it. I wondered if that was what was keeping me going in my new found faith. Did I really want to be a Christian, or just find a way to get back with Joanne?

I could relate to some things in this guy's theory. I'd been through this horrendously hard time and somehow I had found in it that God was real. God worked something bad into something good and I was thankful for it. What if I had been thankful for what He was going to do before the outcome? Maybe there was something to what this author was saying. It was interesting.

CHAPTER 27-"JESUS REVEALED"

The next day, Thursday, I tried to thank God for what had happened to me and Joanne. It was a little strange doing that, seemed like a mind game to me. I wasn't sure about it all, but I felt pretty good through most of the day, which was encouraging. I had been prone to some pretty erratic ups and downs emotionally, depending on how much I was thinking about Joanne.

When I was finished working, Bo and I went to the seafood restaurant for supper. I got the oysters, he had salmon. We finished our meal, got some coffee and settled back in our chairs to just talk. I looked into the bar in the next room and commented to him on how much my activities had changed in the last weeks. I hadn't been in there since the day I met God.

Bo had become somewhat of a mentor to me in terms of Christianity. He always wanted to know how I was doing with God and Joanne, where my head was at. I had told him that I thought God could work out our situation and that's what I was hoping for. He encouraged me, said to keep praying about it. He was good for me at this time, seemed to be keeping me on course. We had a good relationship. Somehow we were able to keep the employer/employee part of our lives separate from our friendship as Christians. He trusted me. He would go home to Juneau on occasion to do some business and visit his family and leave me to run the job. We had hired two more carpenters that had wandered through town one day. They wanted to be in California when winter hit, but would work for us 'til then. We were trying to get the five houses framed and roofed before the snows really hit, which would be sometime in November as I understood from what the townspeople were saying. I still didn't know what to expect from a winter down here. I heard rumors that there would be a lot of rain soon, by mid-October. In Anchorage we didn't see much rain. The snow would be falling soon back there and probably already was creeping down from the peaks of the mountains through the foothills. This place was different, much milder so far.

We finished our coffee and paid our bill. Bo was going back to his trailer to pack a bag and leave for the ferry terminal. He was going home for the weekend. I told him I was going to walk downtown to call Anchorage and see how Joanne and the kids were doing. We said "good-bye" and I headed out the door and down the street toward the center of town. I was tired and turned back around, deciding to go back to my trailer and get my car. I walked the short distance home, got in the car and drove down to Main Street, pulling up in front of a public phone. I looked *at my watch. It was already nine-thirty and getting dark. I wondered if Michelle and Keri would be up. I hurried to the phone booth and dialed the number to Anchorage, dropping in enough coins to talk for about five minutes. Joanne answered the phone.*

"How are you," I asked?

"All right."

"Are the girls still up?"

"Michelle is."

"Let me talk to her."

Michelle came to the phone. "Hi daddy." Her voice sounded strangely detached and sad.

"Hi hon, what's wrong?"

My young daughter cut to the quick, "Daddy, when are you coming home? I want you to come home."

I started to reply my usual "soon", but couldn't get it out. I was choked with emotion. I didn't want to say it, but it came out anyway, "I don't know hon, I don't know. Daddy loves you. As soon as I can I'll be back."

I could hear her crying softly on the line. Joanne got on the phone. There was an unbearable moment of silence that I thought would never end.

"What can I tell her," I asked? "This is so bad."

Joanne said nothing.

"I'll hang up so you can be with her. Tell her what you think is best. Tell her I love her," I added

Some coins tumbled out of the coin-return. The noise jarred me back to where I was. I can't remember any thoughts I had at that moment. I just stood there feeling numb. I had nothing for Michelle that would help her. A feeling of emptiness enveloped my whole being. I was undone. I gathered up the change and staggered like a drunken man to the car, fell into the seat and pulled away from the curb.

By this time tears began streaming down my cheeks. I don't know why, but the theme of the book passed through my mind, "just thank God". Impossible, I was incapable of that, there was no way. I made a right turn up the street by the job. It was starting to get dark. I didn't notice the houses. I didn't notice anything. I was just staring straight through the front window of the car, moving slowly up the street.

I turned up a street to the right again, one I didn't know. It headed back to the street that took you by the bar and downtown. I realized I was going around in a circle and stopped at the corner. I could barely see through my tears. I thought, "I should get off the street, I don't know what I'm doing." My trailer was just a block away, but I didn't want to go there. It was too drab and lonely. Maybe I would go to Terry and Linnus', but decided against it. I didn't want to just show up all upset like this. I wiped the tears from my eyes and looked around to see where I was. There was a church on the corner to my right.

It was dusk now and getting dark quickly, the last embers of daylight were fading into the deepening gray of the night. I could make out a house beside the church and slightly to the rear. I figured that must be the parsonage and saw by the lights from inside that someone was up. The church itself was dark. I wanted to go inside and sit and pray. My instincts leaped with hope at the thought of it. Maybe God would meet me there and help calm my frayed nerves.

I backed the car up to the streetside curb and walked around to the minister's house. I knocked at the back door. An elderly man, who I figured must be the pastor, answered the door. I introduced myself and asked, "Would you mind if I go into the church and sit for a time. I want to pray."

He looked at me quizzically, maybe trying to gauge my sincerity. Apparently he satisfied himself that I was no danger to him or the church and replied, "Sure, that would be alright. I'll open the door for you. Let me get my key. I'll be right back."

He returned and we walked the short distance to a back door that opened into the sanctuary area. "Would you like me to come in with you," he asked?

"No," I said. "I know God," as if that would gain me entrance, like some sort of password to a club, "I just want to sit and pray."

"Okay," he said, "do you need a light?"

"No, that's okay. There's still enough light to see. I won't be too long. Don't worry. I'll be okay. I just need to talk to God. I'll let you know when I leave. Thanks."

He quietly withdrew and left me to myself. I looked around the room to get my bearings. I had come in through a door beside the altar. I didn't know it 'til now, but this was the church where I had been baptized. I recognized the baptismal tank in front of the altar and pulpit.

The rows of pews spread out to the back of the building on both sides of a center aisle. I walked slowly down it and looking toward my left I noticed along a row of windows in the side wall a picture of Jesus. Though it was getting dark quickly now, these windows faced to the west and were the beneficiaries of the day's last light. With its aid I could make out clearly the details of the picture.

It was a large reproduction of a painting, probably three feet high by two feet wide. It was a contemporary work, almost looked like an illustration you might see in a book or Bible, but with no halo over Jesus' head. His face had a very natural look, not pale and saintly, like the old paintings I had seen in museums and churches. His countenance was ruddy, yet kind, his eyes compassionate. He seemed to be looking out of the picture at me. He was climbing a mountain pass, walking its slopes with a lamb slung behind His neck and over his shoulders. You could just make out the features of the landscape behind him, they were blurred in the background. He and the lamb were the focus of the painting as they seemed to walk out directly at you.

I walked up in front of the picture and turned toward it. I stood in the center aisle just staring at it for what seemed like the longest time. Then I stepped forward and kneeled between the rows of pews that were in front of it. I pushed one of the rows back a ways, skewing it so I would have room to kneel. I stayed in that position, on bended knees, for some time more, still staring up at the face which seemed almost alive to me. It was like he was there with me, the image of his picture bringing his presence into the place. The eyes were so warm and kind. I felt as if he knew the pain I had just gone through over Michelle.

I bowed my head before the picture, but really before this sense of his presence in the room. My thoughts began to direct themselves on him. "Who are you Jesus? I want to know you. My friends in church seem to know you. I want to know you too."

I thought about my life, especially about my commitment to find the truth. A conviction that I had done things my way, without regard to him or God or any higher power came upon me in the strongest sense. I felt sorry about it now. I felt as if I had been very stubborn, even wrong for having ignored him. He had been a part of my life as a child and until the experience at the commune three years before he had still held some kind of special place in my thoughts. Though I didn't stop very often to think of him back then, it was more than I had in the last three years, which was not at all. The realization that I had consciously gone my own way pressed in on me like a vice. I couldn't shake the sense of sorrow over it and began to pray out loud, "Jesus," he was so real at that moment, as if I was talking directly to him, "I've gone my own way. You haven't been in any way a part of my life. I'm sorry for that tonight. I want to change that. If you'll show me the way you want me to go from here on out, I'll try to go with you." I bowed my head and began to cry. I meant it, I knew it. That had come from my heart and was sincere. I wanted to know Jesus and wanted to know what he wanted from me.

I remained in that position for I don't know how long. A deep silence in the room, in my mind, in my thoughts, in my soul, seemed to settle over me. It was not a scary thing, nor was it an empty stillness. I knew Jesus was in that room in some form, his spirit, something of him was there. A calm came over me, a sense of peacefulness. It swept aside even the thoughts of the conversation with Michelle, the emotion and heartbreak of all that. I had not read a great deal of the Bible, but something kind of strange happened next. It was almost as if a ticker tape was moving across my mind, like the "big board" tape at Wall Street. I didn't see the words on the tape, but as it moved they came to me. "For God so loved the world that He gave His only begotten Son, that whosoever believes in Him should not perish but have everlasting life." I knew I had read that in the book of John, but I had never memorized it. Yet now I remembered it word for word. A sense of peace filled me from the inside out. Suddenly Jesus Christ was personal to me. I knew that from this moment on I would talk of Him in the same way that my friends did. Something had changed, as if He had walked up and introduced Himself to me. I knew Him now. He was real to me and I had a sense that this was not going to pass. He would stay with me. When the scripture had gone through my mind and I came to the part that spoke about "everlasting life", an understanding that I had never had before came to my mind. I knew that whatever happened in the future, what happened tonight with Him was going to last forever. I knew I was going to Heaven. I seemed suddenly to understand "Heaven" for the first time in my life. I knew I would die, and when I did, I would go there to be with Jesus. All of the questions I had had from hearing my church friends talk about Jesus seemed answered now. I knew who He was, I knew what "Heaven" was, I knew what "eternal life" was. Jesus just switched the light on in my mind and I was different and would never be the same again.

I stayed for a few more minutes, looking back up at the picture. My soul was basking in a peace I had never experienced before in my life. I got up from my knees and walked slowly back toward the door by the altar. I looked back at the picture on the wall two or three times, as if I was afraid He wouldn't come with me when I left. I felt like tonight I was that lamb He was carrying on His shoulder. By the time I got to the door I could barely make out the picture anymore. It had become dark outside during the time I had been there.

I locked the door behind me and crossed the lawn to the minister's house. I knocked on the door. When the pastor answered, the first words out of my mouth were, "I just met Jesus."

"Praise the Lord!", he practically shouted.

His wife walked up behind him as he stood in the doorway, a smile on her face from ear to ear. "We prayed for you son," she said.

"Thank you, it's going to be all right for me now Thank you."

"Do you want to come in," she asked?

"No thank you ma'am. I'm okay. I think I'll just go on home and savor this some more. I'll see you again I'm sure. Thanks for letting me in tonight. You don't know what you've done for me. Thanks."

"All right," the pastor replied, "are you going to church anywhere?"

"Yes, I'm in the church up on the parade ground."

"You're welcome to come here anytime you know, but I'm glad you're going somewhere. Keep that up."

"I will. Good night."

"God bless you son. Come back and let us know how you're doing."

"Okay, I will."

Driving the short distance back to the trailer, I undressed, cleaned up and got into bed. I lay there for a moment just staring up at the ceiling, feeling at peace with God and the world. Now I knew Jesus too. The sense that He was there was overwhelming and I lay quietly taking it all in.

What a change in my life. That my path had somehow been directed since the night I left Anchorage seemed an inarguable fact. God knew where I was even though at the time I hadn't a clue who or what or where He was. Now I did. If only Joanne could know this too. I determined in my mind that I would not give up praying and trying to make this a reality for her. I knew if it could happen to her like it had happened to me, our marriage would be saved. I thought about her back in Anchorage. We were in different worlds now in a way that was spiritual as well as physical. I wondered what it would all mean in the days ahead.

Thinking back now on all the years of searching for truth without finding anything that would last, I knew already that this was different. I had considered many ideas and philosophies but nothing that invaded my experience like God and Jesus had. That was the difference. Jesus was no longer just an idea to me, a figure in history. He was real in my experience, with me, knowing all the details of my life. This was what my friends and I had been looking for back in Massachusetts, when we "turned on" and "dropped out". I had peace with God, a peace that somehow was bringing a sense of meaning and direction to the labyrinth of my life. It all seemed simpler now, much less complex this night.

I hoped that I would be able to someday tell them all about this. I was sure that they would listen to me now that I had something to say. Before I was searching and the words I sang and wrote were a reflection of that effort. Somehow they related to it all, I had struck a chord at times. But I knew I had nothing of substance to give them. I shared their frustration with life and painted a word picture of the struggle. That's why I burnt out, I had nothing to give them or me, nothing to show for the effort, no answers.

Tonight, was different. I had found through my experience of the past month a truth that was inalterable. God was there, He was there all the time. The arrows shot out into the stream of life could find a target in Him. That yearning to find meaning and purpose could be fulfilled, could be found when He was found.

My Bible was on the table by the light beside me. I picked it up and started thumbing through it, looking for the scripture that had been teletyped to my mind's eye when I was praying in the church. I found it in chapter three, verse sixteen of the book of John. I read it again. "For God so loved the world, that he gave His only begotten Son, that whosoever believes in Him should not perish but have everlasting life." The text was exactly as it had come to me in the church. I was amazed. I thought, "this is almost like some sort of personal miracle. I never memorized this." I felt that I was beginning to understand this book, this Bible. At least I knew the meaning of these words and what I had learned this night no one could take from me. What I was reading was inseparably intertwined with what I was living. Nothing I had ever embraced in the past had ever given me such direct experience like this. I seemed then to be reaching for things that were distant. This God I had met, and now Jesus, were near. Though I couldn't see them, I knew they were there. Every moment since I left Anchorage God had been with me. I didn't know that fact when I left. I knew it now. I wondered if He had always been there, before Anchorage, before Alaska, back in Massachusetts, before Joanne, back when I was a child, waiting for me to cry out to Him like I had.

Now, after what had just happened at the church, when I thought of God, Jesus was there too. I couldn't think of One without the sense of the Other being present, they were two persons, yet somehow the

Carl Gove

same. I couldn't separate them. I prayed, "Jesus, just stay with me, like You are with me tonight."

CHAPTER 28-"TONGUES ???"

Still wide awake from the events of the evening I put the Bible back on the night-table beside the bed and picked up the "Prison to Praise" book and decided to read a little more of it before I went to sleep.

The title of the chapter I opened to was "Speaking in Tongues", a subject I knew absolutely nothing about. I couldn't see any connection with the earlier theme about thanking God for everything, but I was curious and read on.

Apparently "tongues" was a phenomenon that was Biblically based. The early disciples of the church first spoke when they were "baptized in the Holy Spirit" at Jerusalem on a Jewish religious holiday called Pentecost. They were in a room praying when the sound of a great wind rushed through the place and they began to speak in languages they had never learned before. Some people, in the city for the holiday, who heard them from outside the room where they were gathered, said they were praising God in languages from the countries where they had come from, although the disciples themselves didn't understand what they were saying when they spoke in these "tongues". The languages they were speaking were unknown to them.

The book went on to say that this experience had, for the most part, left the church by the end of the first century, but resurfaced again in a revival movement around the turn of the twentieth century. People began to be "filled with the Spirit" and "spoke in tongues" like they did in the Bible. At the time of my reading of this book another revival of this phenomenon apparently was taking place. People all over the United States and even the world were being "baptized in the Holy Spirit" and were "speaking in tongues".

The author himself had experienced this and went on to explain that he had sought this "baptism" and understood that when he had asked God to do this in him, that a sign of its having been done would be this ability to speak in another language to God. He said Jesus was the one who baptized us, or "filled us with His Spirit ".

From my reading, I concluded that when it happens, when you ask to be filled, you just somehow believe God and open your mouth and speak whatever God puts there, which would be this new language. He went on to explain what had happened to him, that it sounded silly at first, unintelligible, but why shouldn't it, it was a language you didn't know? But God was doing it, it was in the Bible and even though you didn't understand what you were saying, God did and you could pray and talk to Him with this language whenever you wanted. He said something about the deepest part of you, your spirit, communicating with God directly when you spoke this way.

I understood what this guy was saying, but wasn't terribly attracted to the phenomenon alone. What did it all mean, this baptism, this being filled? If all that it was was this ability to do this "tongues" thing, so what? I put the book down, turned the light out and rolled over, ready to go to sleep. I had met Jesus tonight and now knew who He was. What more did I need than that? Tonight, it seemed that the answer was, "nothing." I faded off into a peaceful and deep sleep. I prayed one last time for Joanne that night, somewhere between waking and sleeping, just before I lost touch with my last thoughts of the day. I had hope in God, and Jesus now, for us. He would work it out. I fell asleep with Him and her on my mind. Why couldn't He just walk up to her and say "hello, I'm Jesus." It would be so easy for Him, but I knew it didn't work that way. I had asked Him to be a part of my life tonight, she would have to do the same.

CHAPTER 29-"THE NASHES"

After work the following day, Friday, I cleaned up and went by Terry's to go to the Bible study, as I had promised him. Over supper I told him all about the night before. He and Linnus were thrilled that it had happened. My story seemed to heighten our conversation through the remainder of the meal. We were all just happy to know Jesus, He seemed to be the centerpiece at the table and in our talk.

We walked up the hill from Terry's back toward my trailer. I didn't realize until tonight that they had been meeting right across the street from where I lived, in a single-story house that seemed to have a lot of windows and I thought that during the day it must be bright with sunshine throughout. One of the living room windows overlooked the bay. As I looked out I could see flashes of nightlights beginning to shine around boats along the dock below the house, as fishermen finished their work for the day. The houses and restaurants and bars along the shore seemed to invite the weary workers to complete their final tasks and retreat to the glow that now shown from within their walls.

The Nashes. Florence and Dwight, greeted me

with warm smiles and a friendliness that made me comfortable from the moment we were introduced. They lived there with their son, Dwight Jr., and their daughter-in-law, Nancy. There were desserts prepared for us to munch on and thankfully, my staple, coffee. After a time of relaxed talking, the eight or so people that had come, migrated to seats around the kitchen table. We began with a prayer, got our Bibles out and had a kind of informal Bible study. Dwight Jr. led the discussion, taking us through some passages in the Old Testament. Everybody was all smiles and serious as he shared, but I didn't have a clue about what he was talking about the whole night and was thankful for the caffeine I was ingesting as he spoke. He talked very quietly and I could feel myself beginning to become drowsy as I tried to listen. Though I wasn't connecting with the study mentally, Dwight was a warm person, with a sensitive manner and tone, and I liked him.

Finally we were finished. After the study they asked if anyone wanted prayer and I asked for Joanne and I, explaining a bit about our situation. Everyone got up and came around where I was sitting. Those closest to me placed their hands on my shoulders and back and head. No one had ever prayed for me like this before in my life. As I bowed my head and listened to the prayers going up to God for me and Joanne and Michelle and Keri, a sense of comfort and caring seemed to be coming through those hands to me. I almost began to tear up. When the prayer was *over and we began to mingle and talk some more, I made a decision that I would come to this meeting on Fridays. A bond seemed to have been made between me and them that night, especially with the Nashes. I was thankful for all of them, Terry, Linnus, Dwight, Florence, Dwight Jr. and Nancy. I could feel their support and it drew me in. After a little more talk I left and walked across the street to my trailer.*

As I lay down to sleep that night I thought, "I know Jesus now, I have some friends, a job, a free place to stay. Under the circumstances, it couldn't be a whole lot better." I was thankful and content as I drifted into another peaceful night's rest.

CHAPTER 30-"THE HOLY SPIRIT REVEALED"

I got up Saturday morning early. My plans were to get some breakfast, go to the church and spend some time in prayer, then work for about half a day. I decided to go to the restaurant down by the docks. It had a nicer atmosphere than the one I normally went to near the job. I drove my car there early, around five-thirty. I brought the book on "tongues" with me and my Bible.

I got to the restaurant, ordered a plate of bacon and eggs and my usual coffee and sat down at a table by a window overlooking the bay and the harbor. It was still predawn and the shadows of night were fading. You could make out the outlines of the mountains in the gray light and in the brighter portion of sky to the west dim patches of snow could be seen contrasted against the darker rocky portions of the mountains' faces. A deep purple hue began to creep down from the peaks of these east-facing slopes where the sun would soon make its entrance on the day. Soon the purple would turn to pink, the pink to orange and the orange to the full light of the day.

Quickly eating my breakfast, I wanted to do some

reading. The waitress poured me another cup of coffee. I picked up the paperback and started the next chapter from where I had left off two nights ago on the subject of "tongues". Now the author was giving a general explanation of what this "baptism" was about. Apparently the phenomenon of "speaking in tongues" was a sign that one had been "filled with the Holy Spirit". Seems I had read that before. Now he talked about a cup that was filled to overflowing, this "baptism" causing our cups to run over with God. Jesus was the baptizer, who would send the Holy Spirit to fill us like this cup, to overflowing, when we asked for this "baptism". When that happened, we would be able to "speak in tongues", talk directly to God in a language we had never learned before. All of this, the "filling", the "tongues", this "baptism" would "magnify Jesus in our lives". That phrase caught me, "magnify Jesus in our lives". I knew nothing about this "baptism" except what I read in this book, but having met Jesus just two nights before, I knew enough about Him, that I would pursue anything that would "magnify" Him in my life. I wanted all of Him that I could get. I determined that I would go to the church and seek this "baptism" right now. More of Jesus, all of Jesus I could experience is what I wanted. If that's what this "baptism" was about, and I had no reason to doubt the truth of what the author wrote, I would go for it.

I paid my bill, got back in my car and drove the short distance up the hill to the church. Using my key, I opened the sanctuary door and went inside. There was just enough daylight coming through the windows to see where I was going, so I went to the front of the church and kneeled on the altar rail where people prayed after a service for some need or request. The rail ran across the base of a raised platform, a stage, on which a pulpit stood at its center, the podium from which the minister would preach. The rail and floor of this stage were designed in such a way that kneeling on the rail, for most people, possibly excepting small children, you could rest your elbows comfortably on the floor of the stage and bow yourself in a position of prayer, which I did. So knowing nothing else than what I had read, I began to pray. "Jesus, I understand that You are the 'baptizer in the Holy Spirit' and that You will fill me with all of You if I ask You to. That's what I want Lord. I want all of You. You've changed me. I want all that You have for me of this new life. Baptize me in the Holy Spirit."

Pausing with my head still bowed I felt no emotion or really much of a sense of His presence, like I had on Thursday. I thought, "This 'tongues' phenomenon is the sign. If I'm filled, I can do that now and I'll know then that He's answered my prayer." I remembered the author talking about how silly his first experience with "tongues" had sounded to him, hearing it with his own ears for the first time, but that you had to open your mouth and believe that God would put a new language there, a language to talk to Him from the deepest part of you, your spirit. Even though you wouldn't understand it, God would, and that's what counted.

So, by the book again, I opened my mouth and spoke a few words of something that was not English. I didn't know if it was any known language, but I knew it wasn't English. I spoke a phrase or two, maybe a dozen words. It was incomprehensible to me. I wondered if I was making it up. I wasn't too impressed, but I believed that this must be it and therefore I was "filled" and Jesus would be "magnified in my life". That's what I wanted and came here for. I waited silently, in my position of prayer, before the Lord, for another moment, then got up to leave.

It was quite a bit lighter in the church now, almost daybreak. In other parts of the town, where the mountains were not in the way, the sun was probably visible to some. Here the high peaks of the bay were directly outside the windows that faced to the east and the sun was behind them yet. But you could see clearly inside the building now, and as I turned to walk away from the altar, down the center aisle of the room, between the pews, I began to feel that peace again that I had felt on Thursday night. I sensed that the presence of God or Jesus or maybe now the Holy Spirit was in the room with me. I stopped and turned back toward the altar, standing midway down the aisle.

A picture of Jesus, another again, was above a table with two silver-colored plates on a simple white *tablecloth centered at the rear of the stage. The picture was the focal point of the entire room. It was a simple reproduction of Him. I had seen it before in other churches I thought, somewhere. He was looking up and out of the frame, not at you. He had a kind and compassionate expression on His face. Uncomplicated as the picture was, it did capture that look.*

I stopped for a moment and gazed at it, and as I did, the sun's first rays broke over the peaks outside of the window just to the right of the altar and stage. It shone through the panes of glass and began to light up the room. As brighter color was added to the wooden pews and carpet and walls of the church, an added dimension of life came to the room and to me. I stood still staring at the picture, the sun rising more and more over the peak, and its light now moving over my body. I had a sense of a warmth like the sun's within me, that, as it rose with each succeeding moment, this warmth rose with it inside me. It was as if I was being filled. It wasn't frightening in any way and as I continued to look at His picture, I felt like Jesus' presence was in this sensation.

An overwhelming feeling of joy, that same kind of joy I felt that day at work when I first felt the presence of God, consumed me and I began to weep openly, still standing in that same spot in the middle of the aisle. I had never experienced in my life "tears of joy", but I felt that that's what these were. I wasn't thinking of Joanne or anything that had anything to do with sorrow. This was a joy I felt inside.

My eyes were still on the picture, though wet with tears now. I thought to myself, "Jesus, You've really changed me. I'm not the same." I realized how true that was and a fresh flood of tears streamed down my face. I had never felt this secure or whole before in my life. His presence seemed to be pulsating in that place.

The windows along the side aisle of the church looked out on the parade ground. On the other side of the open field was the hotel, the former post headquarters. I felt drawn to the windows and walked between the rows of pews to them. Looking out, everything seemed perfectly in place, the lush green of the grass, the deep brown trunks and dark green needles of the pines in front of the hotel and houses that surrounded the open field. I could see the hand of God in it all. I looked over the houses beside the church and could see down the hill to the town below, the roofs of houses and buildings on its other side, back toward where my trailer was, visible in the distance. The thought came to me, almost like a voice from within, "You don't have to be afraid of what's out there anymore. You can be who you are. I'm with you now." More tears came. All seemed right with my life and in the world at this moment. I continued to weep openly.

This ongoing experience of His presence was overwhelming and exhilarating at the same time. I thought, "I'll drive down to the bay, by the beach there." I had been there once before. It's where the road ended. No one lived that far out and I could be alone. I wanted some more time to take this in. Work could wait. I wasn't even thinking about it now.

Jumping into my car I drove quickly by the houses, around behind the hotel and on beyond it to where the road began to wind down behind the town and back toward the water. As I drove fewer and fewer signs of settled life were visible and I was soon in the woods. I crossed an open area, a grassy field above the water, and headed down again through a last stand of pine trees to the bay. In all I had probably driven three miles and descended from the high ground, where the church was, maybe five hundred feet.

This bay was adjacent to the bigger one where the main part of the town was. It was in a westerly direction down the coast, its entrance marked by the peninsula I had just driven down on the one side and across its mouth on the opposite side by the rugged mountain terrain which rose abruptly directly out of the water. It was narrow, maybe one half to three quarters of a mile across. There were no ways to penetrate the western shore, no friendly harbor, no beach, no roads. The beach I was on started from the treeline of the wooded area I had just come out of. It extended along the east shore and began to bend around the water's edge toward the west, where it became more and more narrow until the water, at the head, simply broke against the faces of the slopes rising from its depths. It was a northern beach, no *sunbathers were present or ever would be, no surfers or swimmers either. It was maybe two hundred feet from the trees to the water's edge, where small waves broke quietly along its shore. Pieces of rotting pine logs and driftwood washed in by the waves were strewn at various places in the sand along the way. It was deserted and quiet, only the gentle lapping of the waves against the shore could be heard.*

The sun shone on the water off in the distance to the west. I could see its glittering rays on the crests of the waves as they rolled into the shore. Beyond, across the water, the rocky faces and trees on the mountain walls were fully clothed in their day's light of grays and greens and browns now. On my side, the woods I had just come out of and the beach were still in shadows.

I drove the car as far out on the sand as I could without getting stuck, got out, and walked down toward the shoreline. None of the sense of God's being with me had diminished and when I got to the water, I looked back toward the east and the rising sun. Because of the descent I had made in driving down here, once again I saw the sun break the same peak for the second time that day. I thought, "Two sunrises in one day, that's a first for me."

Soon the shoreline was bathed in its true colors. The water turned from gray to blue. The sand took on its brownish hue. I was on the moist area that had been smoothed by the breaking tide, where it was easier to walk than in the deeper, dryer grains beyond. I was just walking along the beach, feeling as new as the day. That sense of joy was still there.

I began to jog, slowly at first, then my pace quickened. Soon I was running, as if I was in a race. Every few steps I would jump in the air and shout something, I don't remember what, just shouting. A line from an old hymn I recalled growing up in church back in Massachusetts came to me, and as I ran I began singing it out at the top of my voice, "I love to tell the story; 'twill be my theme in glory; to tell the old, old story; of Jesus and His love." I was at my full speed now. I was shouting "thankyou Lord, thankyou Lord" between lines of the hymn.

Still running, I looked to my left out over the water. A bald eagle was gliding just above the waves, at my eyes' level, about fifty feet from me. I could see the outline of his brilliant white crown, his right eye on the side of his head appearing to look right through me. For a moment we were side by side, almost in step with each other, me running, he flying. I began to slow down, just watching him move. He was soon ahead of me and began to rise on a current of wind that left the water below. As he began to ascend I stopped and just watched. My spirit rose with him as he mounted up toward the westward peaks, toward the heavens, closer to God. He soared higher and soon faded in the distance across the water. I lost site of him against the snow on the peaks.

Somehow it seemed as if God Himself had been

watching this scene of a man who had been lost in misery and sorrow running down a beach singing a song with all his heart about a man named Jesus. He seemed pleased with what He saw, His creation even affirming it, the sun rising, the eagle mounting up. I was filled with God that day, filled to overflowing. I had traveled eight hundred miles from my home in Anchorage. I had been gone only a month, yet the distance I had traveled in my soul in that time could not be measured. Like a gospel song I'd heard over the years says it, "I once was lost, but now I'm found; was blind, but now I see." I never knew what they were talking about in that song. I did now though.

CHAPTER 31-"SHARING NEW LIFE"

I walked back to my car and drove back almost dreamily along the road to Haines. I hadn't experienced anything so sublime in all my life. There was no doubt in me that God, Jesus and the Holy Spirit were real. I had met and experienced the Trinity in the past month. What a remarkable odyssey.

As I drove back up through the wooded areas toward Haines, my thoughts drifted to Joanne. I could not give up on this marriage until she either experienced this or made it so clear that it would never happen to her. I had great hope though. I knew that I was like every human being that God loves and that what He had done personally for me He could do for her. He wanted to. I certainly wanted Him to. I would pray and pray until it happened. I was committed to that. I believed already that God could make it all right, Joanne only had to find Jesus.

Heading back by the church I remembered with emotion what had transpired there just a short time ago. I drove down through the town and back to my trailer. I would stop there for a moment and then go on to work.

It looked as though the Nashes were up across the street. I thought, "They would like to hear about this. I'll stop in for a minute." I felt comfortable to do this, even though I had just met them the night before. They seemed like the type of people who would welcome me into their lives and already had made those gestures at the Bible study. I knocked and Florence answered the door with a warm smile.

"Good morning, thought I would stop by and say 'hello'. You know I live just a block up the street on Lynnview."

"Certainly, come on in. We're having breakfast. Can I get you something?"

"Thanks, I ate earlier, but I'll have some coffee if you have some."

"Black, cream and sugar?"

"Black, thanks."

"Go on into the front room while I get it. The Dwights and Nancy are there. I'm glad you stopped by, Carl."

"Okay." I headed into the dining room where the rest of the family greeted me with a genuine warmth. I couldn't get over the friendliness of Christians. I thought, "Were they naive about people, or did they just trust God to protect them from the unscrupulous among us?" They didn't really know me, but they

embraced me nonetheless.

Florence brought the coffee in and we all sat at the dining room table talking amicably. I was right about the house in daytime, the sun streamed through the windows and bathed the inside with a light that seemed to shimmer in every room that it entered.

"I had quite an experience this morning with the Lord. I think I was "baptized in the Holy Spirit" and proceeded to relate the events that had just transpired. It took some time and when I was done, they were all smiling from ear to ear. Dwight Sr. was sobbing openly, a characteristic I would find was common to him. I was comfortable with it, I was prone to tears myself when I felt things deeply and was never embarrassed by them. My father had taught me that. Growing up I had seen him cry and it left a lasting and good impression on me. In a world of male "machismo" that tried to hide tears, my father was an exception. A part of me was always proud of his ability to feel things deeply. I loved my dad particularly for that. I learned humility by watching my dad and knew instantly that in Dwight the same gentle spirit resided

"You know we've all been praying for you Carl. Terry, Linnus, all of us. We feel like we know you well already. Thank God for what he's doing in your life," Florence volunteered

"Amen," I said

"Amen", now there's a word I haven't used for as long as I can remember. Was I becoming a "Jesus freak", a "religious nut"?

The thought that they had prayed for me warmed me. Prayer seemed to bring us closer to God and somehow to each other too. They really did sort of know me already. What a powerful source of communication, to talk to God, a God that heard. In my mind I knew that praying would be the key for Joanne. I thought about the people at the church, about Bo. They had all been praying for me to find God almost since the time they met me. Their prayers had been answered quickly and dramatically. Could I expect the same with Joanne? At the moment I was sure I could. This wouldn't take long. God would save her soon and we would be back together again.

I left for work with that in mind. The events of the morning and that hope buoyed my spirits all that day. I stopped at Terry and Linnus' after work and told them about the morning. They were pleased, in fact had already heard from Florence and Dwight. "These people really care for me," I thought. My conversion was news and a source of strength for them it seemed. What was happening to me was an answer to their prayers and it reciprocated to them by increasing their faith in the Lord.

That night, as I lay down to sleep, I thought that this day couldn't have gone any better. I read a bit from the Bible and continued on in the book on "tongues", said my "goodnights" to the Lord, remembered Joanne and the kids again to Him, and settled into what was becoming a regular occurrence lately, a night of peaceful and contented rest.

CHAPTER 32-"TONGUES REVEALED"

I was up early Sunday morning, looking forward to going to church. I cleaned up and walked to Terry and Linnus' place. The morning was bright and the air was crisp and clear. The warmth of the Indian summer had passed and fall weather was upon us now, it being the first week of October. Colors seemed to blaze at you everywhere, the deep oranges and reds of the oaks and elms, the brilliant blue of the bay in full sunlight, and the emerald green of the pines that mixed with the deciduous trees of the lowland, but grew dominant and covered the landscape as your eyes looked up the slopes that surrounded the town and the bay. The peaks of the mountains displayed a newly laid blanket of pure white snow, which would soon find its way down the rocky faces, along the forest floors to the valleys below, as the temperature continued its descent into winter.

Terry, Linnus and I had agreed the night before to meet and walk together to church that morning. Dwight Jr. and Nancy were there when I arrived at their place and the five of us headed off together. I looked forward to the service after what had happened yesterday. Church was becoming an event I always anticipated now. I remembered growing up it was mostly a chore.

We sang some hymns, some of which I would remember from my youthful years. I sat next to Nancy and noticed she could really sing. Singing was something I always enjoyed too and some said I had a decent voice. We sang "Holy, Holy, Holy", a hymn I knew. As I sang the expression on the page seemed charged with truth about God and I found myself singing louder than I normally had before in church. The Holy Spirit's presence seemed to be there in a special way: I looked up at the picture which the day before had such a significance and I wanted to tell the Lord how thankful I was for what He had done. Somehow singing about His holiness seemed to accomplish that this morning.

Even Don's preaching seemed especially charged to me. I listened intently, not wanting to miss a word or change an intonation. Somewhere between sermon points, I decided that I would take a ride after the service. Since I had made that special drive out of Canada when I came here I had determined to someday go back to the pass and climb one of the mountains. If I left right after the service, I could do it this afternoon and be back for church that night.

As soon as the service was over, I told Terry my plans and headed straight out to walk back to the trailer, get my car and go.

I headed out along the highway going north, past

the saw mill and out along the river which headed toward the mountains of Canada. I noticed more eagles, along the river bed on this trip, some molting. Apparently they had become impregnated or were preparing to, though they weren't putting their best dress on if that were the case. Their feathers, rather than the dignified deep brown color and brilliant white crown we're all so used to, were dappled gray and white. Not very glorious or attractive.

This area was so abundant with the birds though. Some of the large trees along the way, which had begun to drop their leaves for the winter, revealed dozens of them perched upon their branches, eyeing the river below for signs of life that they could prey upon for their survival.

As I climbed out of the river valley into the pine forests on the slope of the ascending range, the beauty of the road had lost some of its intensity for me as well. I guess that first trip, that first view of a new area, like the first special look of love, is always the most succinct and memorable. The perfection in time and place seemed to have faded, though the appreciation, not charged with the same initial raw emotion, still remained. It had deepened somewhat to something more decided, an affirmation of the beauty and touch of the Creator's hand on this place.

I passed through the customs station and on up above the tree line to the valley which defined the pass going on into Haines Junction and the Yukon's *vastness beyond. I parked the car off the gravel road, along its side, picked a peak to climb, crossed the road and began my ascent. I estimated I would have a climb of approximately five to six hundred feet over mostly rocky terrain to a summit which was bare of any signs of snow. I managed it without much difficulty and within the hour was at the peak.*

I had carried my Bible along with me, and found an outcropping of rock that had a flat spot where I could sit. The mountains stretched out as far as I could see to the south and west, miles of unencumbered peaks and high valleys, inaccessible to man's footsteps and inroads. In the distance you could see where they dropped off abruptly toward the coastline below, which from my position was not discernible except in the remote distance where the mountains reached like fingers out into the vastness of the coastal waters which shimmered like a mirage on the horizon.

I could see my car directly below me, a red dot on the gray gravel of the road. The other side of the pass, rose across the road directly in front of me. To the east, I could see the route cutting and winding its way inland to the scattered pockets of settlement in this wilderness sea which was the northland

I had decided to read a passage or two of my Bible up here where I must surely be closer to God. My thoughts would be clear and unhindered from these heights. I would have a view of things from His perspective on high.

I was finishing the first book of the New Testament, Matthew, which I had started after completing my reading of John. It was the story of Jesus' life, like John's book, but with some different perspectives and highlights. Jesus had just been resurrected from the grave and had appeared to His disciples on a number of occasions. He was now heading home to God and at the end of the book, His disciples were standing in a group looking up at the place where they actually saw Him rise into the sky above. He had left them with some comforting words and angels appeared after He had left their sight and told them that He would return again someday as they had seen Him go, riding upon the clouds. It seemed like an emotional scene. The disciples had seen Him die, rise from the dead, appear to them and now leave again within the last month. Their moods must have been on a roller coaster ride. A lot of what they were experiencing they didn't fully understand at the time. I could see that in reading this now.

I finished the book and placed the Bible down on a rock beside me. I started thinking about this book, the Bible. A book which for most of my life had meant very little to me was now important. I was thankful for that. I decided to kneel and thank the Lord for His book. I did that and began to thank Him for all of the other things He had been doing in my life. Without thinking about it, I started to "speak in tongues". Remembering the book I had read, that it was a prayer language that I could talk to God with, I began to speak again, like the morning before at the church. The book had said even though you didn't understand what you were saying to Him, your spirit, the deepest part of you, was communicating with Him and He understood.

I continued to pray in "tongues". The words just seemed to flow of themselves. I was fully conscious and heard what I was saying. I knew I could stop whenever I wanted to. Though I seemed to be repeating some phrases, I had a sense that I was speaking cognizantly and putting phrases together that made sense, that had a beginning, middle and end.

I must have prayed this way for close to half an hour. A stopping point just seemed to come and opening my eyes I looked around having almost forgotten where I was. The side of the mountain seemed steeper than when I had started, and I felt a little dizzy and unstable, like I had to catch myself to prevent rolling down. When I regained my equilibrium, I had this sense about my prayer, that even though I didn't understand what I had said to the Lord, I had unloaded my insides completely, a "deep-cleaning". A weight of care and burden seemed to have lifted off my shoulders. I wondered if I had prayed for Joanne somehow. A great sense of that peace that I was beginning to experience so often now overwhelmed me. I felt as though this phenomenon I was experiencing for the first time would be something I ought to draw on as I continued to pray and talk to God. I knew I had connected with Him.

I headed back down the mountain and to my car. It was four-thirty and I would have to step on it to get back for church at six o'clock. I got there just in time and cleaned up a little. My church clothes were my work clothes, casual clothes and now dress clothes. They were all I had, jeans, a tee-shirt and work boots. That was me, the Alaskan carpenter. Nobody seemed to care, though they dressed up much more than I did. They were more concerned with my being there than they were with how I looked. I never had anyone, in fact, tell me to clean up my act or anything like that. The Lord seemed to be taking care of that on His own. The congregation didn't step in His way.

Not many people came on Sunday nights. Sunday morning was the largest crowd of the week. Both Sunday nights and Wednesdays were sparse. In all there were about eighty people in the church, if everyone showed up Sunday mornings. The evening services, thirty max.

Don would share a short message Sunday night. Before he began though, he would open up the service to anyone who wanted to tell people about something that had happened to them that week, something the Lord had done in their lives that was significant. They called this a "testimony" and the time in the service was referred to as "testimony time". I had never involved myself in this before, though many significant events were occurring in my life. I was never uncomfortable about speaking with people or even in front of people, just hadn't participated before tonight.

I wanted to tell people about being "filled with the Spirit". I thought about it. I couldn't tell them everything about yesterday, it would take too long. I thought, "I'll tell them about this afternoon on the mountain and 'speaking in tongues'." That would be something they could all relate to and it would probably make them feel good that I was now "Spirit-filled".

I raised my hand. Don acknowledged me and I got up from my seat. "Yesterday, I got 'filled with the Holy Spirit' here at the church. I came to pray early in the morning. Today, after the service, I took a drive back into Canada, up in the pass, climbed a small mountain along the road there, and when I was praying to the Lord, I 'spoke in tongues' for maybe half an hour. It was a great experience for me and I'm sure it's something all of you probably do already. I know I want to do it more when I'm praying."

Usually when people shared "testimonies", when they were finished, you could hear a chorus of "praise the Lord" from others in the congregation. Not so with this one, and I didn't understand why. Terry was there and had a troubled look on his face. I didn't get it.

The service ended and Don came up to me and asked me to come over to the house for a moment. I said "sure" and when everyone left I headed next door. He and Wilma were there waiting for me. Wilma made some coffee and Don and I sat down at the kitchen table.

Don had a look of fatherly concern on his face and opened up the conversation, "Carl, about your testimony, it may not be the Lord that's inspiring what's happening here in your life."

"What do you mean", I asked?

"Well, we're Baptists. We don't believe that you get 'baptized in the Holy Spirit' in the way you described. We believe that you get 'filled with the Spirit' when you get 'saved'. You don't need to ask for it like you did or 'speak in tongues' to verify it."

"Wait, I don't understand. You don't believe in what's happened to me?"

"No, we don't. Not all Christians believe the same on the 'baptism'".

"So, if what happened to me yesterday didn't come from God, then where did it come from?"

"The Devil," Don emphatically replied.

"What?"

"The Devil often tries to deceive young Christians."

"I don't know what you're talking about, I don't know anything about the Devil. You're saying that what happened to me yesterday came from the Devil?"

"Yes, I am."

This explained the reaction I got back in the service when I shared about my experience with "tongues". I was totally thrown for a loop by this. My emotions were a jumble. If what I experienced yesterday and today was a trick, a lie, how could I be sure of anything I'd gone through in the last month? Was any of it real? I slumped in my chair and put my head in my hands. I couldn't make any sense of the thoughts that were coursing through my mind at the moment. I was totally confused and upset by his words. Where would I go from here? How could I make sense of this now?

I weakly replied after an anguished moment, "How could anything that was so good, so life-changing to me, be evil? I don't understand you Don. I'm back to square one. I don't know what to think anymore about any of this."

Don sat in silence, not knowing how to respond to me. Wilma was standing off in another area of the kitchen, silent too. We all remained speechless like that for about thirty seconds, but it seemed longer, interminably longer. My Bible was in front of me on the table. I looked up at it, not for any reason, it was just in my path of sight. I stared blankly at it as it sat silent too.

A thought trickled into my mind. I spoke, "If this

is from God, there must be something about it in this book, something that explains what's happened to me."

Don still hadn't offered any thoughts. He looked almost sad, sitting across from me. He knew I was devastated by what he had said

I flipped open the cover, not because I wanted to read anything right now, it was just kind of a knee-jerk reaction to my comment. On the pages of the Bible I had there were headings that gave a reference to what was in the section you might be reading. The references were to particular events or topical. My eyes fell on the heading of the page I opened to. It said "Speaking in Tongues".

I nearly came out of my seat. I exclaimed, almost shouted, "Look at this, 'Speaking in Tongues', right here, right on this page."

Don seemed to jump in the seat he was sitting in. I couldn't see Wilma, standing behind me, or her reaction. I saw that I was in the book of Corinthians. I glanced over the chapter, chapter 14, to see what it said. I saw phrases like "my spirit prays to God, though my understanding is unfruitful", "I will pray in the Spirit and I will pray in the understanding", "I would that you all speak in tongues". I thought back to the afternoon on the mountain. I could relate what this was saying to my experience there.

"Here it is! This is what happened to me this

afternoon. I prayed in English, I prayed in 'tongues'. I didn't know what I was saying, but I knew that I was making contact with God, from the deepest part of me. This is from God, everything's okay! Man, this is something, it's right here in the Bible, amazing."

I don't remember what Don said after that, if he said anything at all. It's as though he couldn't argue with how the conversation had literally unfolded and resolved itself in a way that gave me a sense of assurance and confidence in what I had gone through in the last two days.

I left shortly after that and drove slowly back to the trailer from the church. I couldn't get over how the Lord was there when I needed Him tonight. He cleared up all the confusion in my mind in an instant. The Bible seemed to be more than a book now. Somehow God interacted in its words and pages and with the events of my life. It was as if it was breathing and alive. The Lord used it in a direct way to help me through something I didn't know how to deal with. I placed it on my nightstand with a newfound respect and as I faded into sleep, I "prayed in the Spirit and in the understanding" for one last time that day. I knew what was happening to me was coming from God and would not question it again.

CHAPTER 33-"HOPE"

One month later, the clocks had been turned back and winter was close at hand. It had been raining continually for days on end, the sun only occasionally breaking through the clouds to light the land below in a temporal display of color, only to be shrouded again by layers of gray.

Early on I had tried to wait out the rain before working on the houses, but had soon capitulated and purchased a full set of rain gear. My saw cords seemed to be soaked through the protective coat of insulation and from the roofs of the houses I was framing I apprehensively traced them back down the walls of the house and across the puddled lots to the power pole out on the street. I thought at any moment during the day I could become a Christmas tree, but if I wanted to eat, I had to work in this. The rain seemed like it was never going to subside. Someone humorously joked that they saw the local wildlife walking two-by-two down the road to the ferry terminal where they boarded a large wooden boat awaiting them there.

I was by this time firmly established in my new Christian lifestyle. Jesus had become by far the most important relationship in my life. I knew other people would probably regard me as a "fanatic", but to me it wasn't that way at all. After what He had done in my life, it seemed only natural to want to put Him first and make Him a priority in my thinking and activity.

I was at church whenever they opened the doors, Sunday mornings, Sunday evenings and Wednesday nights. Also, I went to the Bible study on Fridays at the Nashes. I was reading regularly through the Old and New Testaments, two chapters in the old and one in the new every day. I also read a daily devotional and prayed each morning before going to work. I listened to teaching tapes and pretty much talked "God-stuff" constantly with my friends, with Bo, with Don. I was a confirmed "tongues talker" now too. I had become comfortable with this language God had given me to pray with and like the Bible says, "I prayed in the Spirit (in tongues) and I prayed in the understanding (in English}. When I couldn't find the words to express myself in English to the Lord, somehow "tongues" seemed to meet that need.

I often prayed in "tongues" with Joanne on my mind. I have no idea if I was really praying for her, but I was praying intently and assumed that some of what I was saying may have related to our situation. These prayers in "tongues" and prayers in English were becoming a big part of my life and throughout the day, not just in the morning, but whenever she came to my mind (which was often), at work, at church, in the evening before I went to sleep, I would say her name before the Lord and ask Him to move in her life in the same way He had moved in mine. I believed without any doubt that He could make the difference in our marriage. He was the element that our relationship lacked and He wanted and would restore her and my children to me. I lived day to day now with that hope.

When I left Anchorage I didn't really think that we could make it, though I desperately wanted to. I remembered that night at the bar, when I was thinking about the future and had to reluctantly admit that the probability of our reconciling was not there. Now I believed it was entirely possible with the Lord. I was living for that. I listened to cassette tapes of true stories of people whose marriages had been restored by Jesus. I read books. I memorized scriptures that gave me hope in that regard. I was focused in every way on it. The Bible seemed to be full of promises that assured me if I prayed and believed God, it was His will to put us back together again.

I was talking to Joanne fairly regularly. She had a car that we had when I was there, an old clunker, but it ran. She had taken a job at the airport out by our apartment, working in one of the restaurants in the terminal. I was sending her money nearly every week, so she was doing okay financially, as far as I knew.

I naturally was telling her about the changes in my life. I told her, "This is what we were looking for back home. This is real peace, inner peace, peace with God." It amazed me that when I was a writer and didn't have an answer to any of life's questions, people seemed to hang on every word I said, as if I knew something. Now that I had found something that was real, no one wanted to hear about it. I was a "Jesus freak" now, a "religious fanatic". I think that's what Joanne thought, and she believed that it would pass. I had had religious enthusiasm in the past, and after a time my zeal for a particular path faded and I was on another. Her being skeptical about my latest revelations was understandable after only a month and a half. Church was not a place she had any desire to be. She seemed happy with her circumstances, her freedom. It was what she was looking for when she made the break with me.

I would have been better off if I talked more with God about my wife and less with her. I tried hard to convince her over the phone, but the change she had gone through was in a direction she wanted to go and for the moment she was happy with it. For me there was only the unhappiness. I never wanted the change, she wanted her's. Maybe I had more of a disposition to soul-search at the time than she, because the life that I had and still wanted had fallen apart. She wasn't searching for answers, nor was I when I left, but I was in a different frame of mind because I didn't want the separation.

I have a stubborn, hard-headed way about me when I'm trying to convince someone of something. I can drive a person to a point where they just want to *be away from me. I was doing that with her. She was probably grateful that eight hundred miles was between us after some of our arguments over the phone. I should have backed gracefully off, but I didn't and was probably giving her a lousy impression of what Christianity was all about. I am sure I was coming across as a "fanatic". I wanted to give a good impression of what had happened to me and I wasn't. She probably didn't have a clue what was going on. I never told her any of the story, the events that had occurred with me. I just told her in so many words, "You need this! Why don't you get with it?" This was not good, not helping. In my zeal for "all things God", I didn't know how to back off I had hope for us now, coming from my relationship with Jesus, but had so much to learn about His way of communicating what I had found.*

CHAPTER 34-"HE SPEAKS"

In my times of optimism and high hope I had a belief that God would work out our circumstances for good, that He would restore us to each other, that the marriage would not dissolve but survive, that our home with our children would be restored. That hope was a sort of bedrock in my soul, yet often in my outward appearance that was not apparent. The trappings of my shifting emotions often clouded it and drowned it out. A word on the telephone, a letter, a sad thought, often dominated what I was feeling and it was a struggle daily to stay up and focused on the Lord and on that hope. I had periods of discouragement that I couldn't pull myself out of, countered by others of encouragement that carried me on waves of optimism for the future.

That was my life. Work was there, church was there, my friends were there, and always Joanne was on my mind, a thought away from what I was doing at anytime. Physically we had left each other, but in every other way she was still with me.

I expected quick results on the Lord's part. I thought that at any moment I would get a phone call or a letter asking me to come home, telling me she miraculously went by a church and heard a preacher talking about Jesus and prayed that He would come into her life, or that someone she worked with would tell her about the Lord and she would break down and pray. I continually imagined scenarios like this. None of them happened and no phone call, letter, or conversation gave any indication that it was going to happen soon. I didn't understand and I kept running across Bible verses about patience, endurance, longsuffering and such that I didn't like. How long would this take? When would God move?

My life cycled between these ups and downs. The Lord was always with me though. When I would hit a down mode, some scripture, some word in a message or a song from church, something Terry, Dwight, Florence or Bo might say, would breathe a breath of fresh hope to my flagging emotions.

It was a Friday in November. The houses were pretty nearly framed in, with plywood on the roofs, ready for shingles or hot mopping, whichever the case. Bob had gone his way. I kind of missed him. He was a kind-hearted guy. He had come to church and really took a look at what was there, but for whatever the reason, never really made the commitment to find out more. We had become pretty good friends. He understood the changes I had gone through and that probably spoke more than any words I could put forth in an argument to try to convince him of his need to know Jesus. I thought about him a number of times after he had left and prayed for him.

Bo and I finished work about four-thirty. It was getting dark close to five o'clock now. The day had been on the gloomy side, gray clouds hovering over the bay. Only the lower slopes of the mountains coming up out of the water could be seen in the shroud of clouds. We were socked in. There would probably be a storm that night. We had already seen two snowstorms that month. The temperature was dropping with each passing day and the snow would soon be here to stay. Between the first and second storm, the snowfall had melted and more winter rain had fallen. From here on out though it would be cold enough that we wouldn't see any rain until spring.

Storms were more frequent down here than in Anchorage. The temperature was generally warmer, though the cold seemed to penetrate more with the moistness of the air. Southeastern Alaska was a rainforest, and though it was beautiful when the sun shone and the sky was clear, according to the locals, these frequent storms would be the norm until spring. Only for a short time during the summer did the weather really clear for any extended period.

We went to the restaurant by the bar, our favorite dinner place in Haines. From where we usually sat, you could see out over the bay. We would often eat and sit and talk after a day's work. It was relaxing for both of us. I had my usual plate of oysters and was drinking a cup of coffee, looking out over the water. I was feeling depressed today, probably the weather added to it some. The evening shadows were beginning to obscure the view and street lights were beginning to show the way for those who were still moving about the town, heading home or to the bars for the evening.

"You're quiet tonight Carl," Bo ventured.

"Yeah, I know."

"I know what you're thinking about."

"It's hard not to. Why hasn't God done something? What possible good can come of this separation from her or the kids?"

"She has to come to a place where she realizes, like you did, that she needs something more in life."

"I know. It's still hard. I'm lonely. I miss her. It hurts."

"You've got to keep trusting the Lord. He wants marriages to work."

His words sounded kind of empty and trite tonight. I knew that what he was saying was true, but I was really wanting to throw a pity-party for myself.

"I'm going to head home. The Bible study at the Nashes is later. I'm going to rest a little in the trailer before I go. I'll see you in the morning."

"All right, have a good night Carl."

"See you." I headed out the front and walked up

the street toward the trailer. There was a light in the Nash's kitchen. Florence was probably getting ready for us later, making cake or cookies or something. I could see Dwight at the kitchen table with a cup of coffee. I was in no mood to stop, though I had become close with them and could come and go in their house unannounced.

Bo didn't go to the study on Friday with me. It was peopled by those of us who believed in the "Baptism" and who had experienced "speaking in tongues" and being "filled". There was another church in the area, in fact the one I went to the night I prayed to Jesus for the first time, that taught the "Baptism". They were called Pentecostals. I had thought about going there since I believed differently on that subject than the Baptist church I attended, but I was close to everyone in my church. I had more or less grown up there since coming to the Lord. Terry, Linnus, Dwight and Nancy all went there and no one ever asked me to leave because of what had happened to me in regard to "tongues". Don and I continued to talk about our differences from time to time but it never became a divisive issue between any of us. They were committed to me and wanted to see me grow and wanted to see me get back together with Joanne. So I was content to stay in the church I was at.

It was almost completely dark when I unlocked the door to the trailer. I groped around on my way in for a light. Over the short walk from the restaurant to home, I kept digging a deeper hole of depression over my circumstance. Seeing Dwight and Florence as I passed by their window had sent a sharp pain to my heart. Here was a family together and here I was alone, eight hundred miles from my own.

"Why," I asked myself and God?

I found my way to the back of the trailer where my bedroom was and flicked a switch which lit a single overhead ceiling light. The room looked barely lit up. It seemed dull and lifeless, my sleeping bag on a makeshift plywood bed, no mattress, a paltry wooden crate for a nightstand with a small reading light on it, a small portable space heater which needed to be on continually when I was in the place now that winter had arrived. My clothes were stacked in my only suitcase in the comer. This was my life. Everything in the place seemed so meager. I felt the same. Here I was hoping in a God I couldn't see or hear, someone I just believed was there. For a moment a twinge of doubt seemed to slip into my mind and I wondered, "Was this hope I had for Joanne and I doing me any good?" Looking at this room at the moment didn't do much to reassure me that it was.

I felt an anger at the situation coming up inside me. I was frustrated with my life. It seemed senseless and of no account. I slammed my hand against the thinly paneled wall of the room. The whole trailer shook it seemed from the force of the blow.

"Lord, this stinks! Why don't You do something? I've been here four months now." I could visualize this *stretching into six months and then a year and longer. "I'm lonely, I miss my wife, I miss my kids. My kids miss me. I'm here alone, she's there. I hate this! It stinks! Why don't you do something?"*

I fell on the floor by the side of my bed and began to weep. I was angry at God. I looked up at the ceiling and raised my hands toward Him in an agony. I got up from the floor and hit the wall again. I was getting out of control. I wanted to hit something again, as hard as I could. I looked around the room for something, anything.

On a table by the nightstand was a small portable tape recorder plugged into the wall by the bed. I had been listening to teaching tapes on the Bible, amongst other things. I remembered that Florence had given me a tape about a man who had been separated from his wife like me, but who had been restored to her after he and she had come to the Lord. I thought, "You did it for them. What about me and Joanne? It's been almost five months and You're not doing anything!", and again I cried, "I hate this! It stinks! What good is this doing me or her or my kids?"

Raising my left hand high over my head I brought it down as hard as I could on the table in a karate type motion. I hit the recorder as my hand slammed down. The side of my hand hit the row of control switches along the bottom edge of the recorder. The machine almost came up off the table from the impact of the blow and as it landed back upon the tabletop, the tape came on. The first words that came out of the recorder, with sufficient volume that I could clearly hear them were, "God is going to restore your home."

I didn't remember from the last time I had heard the tape what context those words were being spoken in. It didn't matter. I didn't hear anything that was said after that either. The words seemed to echo in the caverns of my mind and in the room again, "God is going to restore your home."

In my despair, the Lord spoke. I froze in my place and stared blankly at the wall. Tears were now streaming down my cheeks again. I switched off the recording. "God is going to restore your home." Again, the words coursed through my mind.

I collapsed to my knees in the middle of the floor, my face pressed against it, groaning in response to the impact those words were having on me. The anger ran out of my body like a flood. I thought, "This is God, who am I to get angry with Him, to question His ways?" I felt ashamed and extremely sorry for what I had been feeling towards Him.

"Father, forgive me! Forgive me Lord You know what's happening with me. You care. I'm sorry. Forgive me for doubting You, for questioning You. I'm sorry Lord, I'm sorry."

CHAPTER 35-"TRUST"

November had passed and winter was in full throat now in Southeast Alaska. Snow was on the ground and piling up. Christmas was coming soon and I planned on returning to Anchorage after the New Year holiday, but as the time neared to go, the bands on my old Chevy automatic transmission began slipping. There was a mechanic in town, John, who had an old experienced transmission specialist named Oley, a Swede, that worked with him and I brought the car to them for repair. He tried twice tightening the bands but to no avail. Each time I would take the car for a test-drive they would start slipping again. I could in no way handle an eight hundred mile drive to Anchorage with a car doing that. Time was passing. It was close to February now and I was so disappointed. Wanted to get back to Joanne and the kids so badly even though we would still be separated. Less distance though if I was there.

John, Oley and I decided to order a rebuilt transmission from Seattle which came early in the last week of January. John and I joked about blindfolding Oley to see if he could still put it back in. This was the third time he had removed and reinstalled one on my car.   It was late Friday afternoon when the work was finished without any hiccups along the way. I test drove it and everything seemed fine. I would leave the next morning, finally. I was excited. Oley and John were packing away tools, closing the shop for the weekend and all was well. I had paid them some extra money above the cost of the rebuilt. They probably hadn't made anything on the job, but they were happy that it was done and wished me well with my family back in Anchorage.

I said "goodbye" and headed down to Terry's. I didn't even get to his house before the bands started slipping again. I pulled the car over to the side of the road and laid my head on the steering wheel. I pounded on it a couple of times in frustration. After a minute or two I decided to bring it back to the garage. John was just leaving when I pulled up. I told him what happened. With a resigned sigh he told me to bring the car around back and park it. He would call Oley and have him take out the transmission in the morning. We would get another one from Seattle. The one I had must have been a "lemon" he thought. He showed a lot of tolerance under the circumstances. This must have been as hard on him as it was on me. We said goodnight. I told him I'd bring the coffee and doughnuts in the morning. The least I could do.

I walked downtown to the restaurant and sat over a cup of coffee for about an hour. My mind was numb. I wanted to go home so bad. I left my lukewarm cup and walked to a pay phone outside and called Joanne.

"Unbelievable," she said, "I'll have to tell the girls again."

"I don't imagine they'll understand, they just want me to come home."

"Yeah, it will be all right. Do you want to talk to them?"

"You tell them, I'll call tomorrow or Sunday. It's going to be another week and a half at least."

"Okay, let me know."

"Yeah, goodbye."

"Bye."

I walked up by the garage and over to where my car was sitting outside. One and a half months of car work. "Why, Lord? Just let me get home." I was anxious about it all. I walked up to the car and laid a hand on it and prayed that the Lord would fix it without the mechanic, just make it work, heal it like He healed people in the Bible. It was ridiculous, but I just wanted to go. I felt as though my life was on hold. I wanted control of it again. I knew I wasn't really trusting God in all this. Maybe there was a purpose that I didn't understand in God's providence for all this delay. I was being broken by the circumstances that forced me to wait. Did God just want me to give Him control and trust Him? He had my attention. Was I fighting against His hand? I just wanted to go, the sooner the better. My insides seemed to be shouting, "Let me go Lord, let me go." I wondered for a moment if I was ready for what was ahead. The timing of my going was in God's hand. If He wanted it, I would have already been there. Was hard for me to trust that though. Still young in all of this.

I headed for the Friday night study. No one could believe what happened with the car again. They told me to keep trusting. The words seemed empty at the moment. I asked them to pray that I would not fight the circumstances as hard as I had been, that I'd be able to give the situation more to the Lord and be at peace about everything that was going on. That word again, "trust". I was tired of hearing and thinking of it for the moment, but knew it was what I needed.

CHAPTER 36-"ON THE ROAD AGAIN"

The car wasn't miraculously repaired. Two weeks later, it was now nearly the end of February. I was finally ready to leave. I stayed in town an extra two days just to be sure the bands weren't going to slip on the new transmission. Everything seemed okay and I began to say my goodbyes to all the friends from church and elsewhere I had made in Haines. Everyone assured me that their prayers would be with me and Joanne. I was a bit nostalgic about leaving.

The Friday Bible study group had a special meal for me Thursday night at the Nashes. They all gathered around me and prayed for me one last time, some laying their hands on my shoulders while they prayed. I felt the blessing of having been among them these last seven months. They had helped me find and get started with the Lord. Bo and Don and Wilma came this night, even though they knew we were the group that believed in "tongues" and all that stuff. They put their differences aside for the moment to wish me well. They had impacted me and I had impacted them too. To see the transformation in my life was an encouragement to their faith in Jesus. He could still

185

change lives, of which I was a living proof.

Friday morning was as bright and clear and cold a winter's day as Alaska had to offer. There wasn't a cloud in the sky. I could feel a slight, tingling pain in my chest as the cold air from a deep breath hit my lungs. Florence cooked me a big breakfast of bacon, toast, eggs, juice and the staple of my diet, coffee. Terry and Linnus came by. Dwight Sr. was in tears as he hugged me at the door. He, Florence, Dwight Jr., Nancy, Terry and Linnus, and Bo stood by my car as I pulled away from what had been home for the last seven months. I looked across the street at the trailer and back the other way at the Nash's house. Don and Wilma had driven down again from the church. I embraced all of them one by one, to the sounds of "God bless you" and "we'll be praying". They all were standing and waving now in my rearview mirror. I waved out my window for the last time and turned down the street towards downtown. I could see the bay sparkling in the morning sun in the distance and the church across and up the rise on the other side of town. The gables of the hotel roof on the parade ground jutted through the trees in the distance. I felt tears running down my cheeks and thanked the Lord for this place. So much had happened to me here. My incubator with Jesus. I wondered if I ever would see it again. It would always be special to me.

CHAPTER 37-"THE YUKON IN WINTER"

I headed north out of Haines for the last time, past the restaurant I ate at before finding the job with Bo, past the houses where Charlie and Faith and others from the church lived, past the sawmill where Terry worked, it was all familiar to me now.

Soon I was driving along the river bank, through the valley that would lead up and over the pass in Canada. What had been arrayed with color in the late summer when I arrived was now simply covered with a blanket of pure white snow. The river was frozen over in spots and molted eagles walked along the edges of the ice, scavenging for remains of fish along the banks. In the oaks and hemlock trees on the opposite side of the road, stripped bare now of any leaves, they could be seen on every branch of every tree I passed. They were so dense in one tree, that I stopped to count. I was at sixty-five when I stopped, and there were many more, probably over one hundred. Some people never get to see a bald eagle in their lives and here I was gazing upon one hundred of them on one tree.

All that was visible looking up the slope of the

foothills to the north was a carpet of snow that covered completely the forest floor. Further up, the tops of the pine trees shown a deep green contrasted against the white. At the very top of the mountains, some rock outcroppings could be seen jutting out from the snow-smoothed and rounded peaks. Above was the bright and brilliant blue of the sky, clear and almost crystalline. It sparkled against the white of nearly everything below it.

On a day such as this, clear, without a cloud cover, the temperature drops to its lowest points. I was glad that the heater was blowing out its warm air and hoped that the repairs I had spent so much time and money on would hold up in the Yukon ahead of me. I had never traveled in the dead of winter like this and if the sky remained this clear, I knew that the temperature there would be well below zero throughout the day. I would have to know where roadside stops were and carefully gauge my gas between them. If anything were to happen to the car and the heat it provided me I might just as well be transported back two hundred years for all the worth the wonders of the twentieth century would be for me in the middle of the Yukon wilderness in winter. I really wasn't prepared for that. Hindsight is twenty-twenty. I was a bit foolish and naive about traveling this time of year. There would be little traffic on the road. I had mistakenly counted on traffic more than I should have in my preparation. The further I got away from Haines, the more I realized what a thin line existed between me and the elements. I tried not to think about it.

I passed the border checkpoint, where the Canadian Mountie quizzed me on my destination and when I expected to be leaving Canada. I told them I was driving straight through to Anchorage and would probably be at the U.S. border by five or six o'clock. As I pulled away from the tiny stationhouse and headed up toward the pass I thought to myself that they probably alerted the northern border of my presence on the road. If I didn't show up within some reasonable time after my stated intention, they would start a search for me along the highway. Driving the AlCan was serious business in winter.

I broke out above the tree line and wound up to the pass. The wind was blowing and swirling the snow along the ground and across the highway as I drove. What had been beautiful and inviting in the summer now looked perilous and foreboding. I was thankful to arrive in Haines Junction and stopped for a cup of coffee and to fill my tank with gas. Everything was different, the town, the road, the scenery all seemed to be in hibernation, storing up its treasure until the spring would bring its warmth.

When I got out into the wide-open spaces of the Yukon tundra, there were only two colors to be seen, the white of the earth and the blue of the sky, nothing else. My heater was going full bore and I could still feel the cold penetrating the car. The land looked like *a block of ice, the snow crystals themselves seemed to be frozen together in a lump. I could hear the wheels crunching over the road, which was only discernible as a width of packed powder winding through the mounds of white on either side of its boundary. On a cloudy day, or in a storm, this area would be in "whiteout" conditions. You wouldn't have been able to find the road. An occasional stake marked its sides, sticking up noticeably in contrast to its surroundings. I was thankful for the clear weather, but wondered if I would be able to travel at night on a road like this. I was thankful too to see the occasional roadside lodge, where you could get food and gas and conversation. It was good to hear another voice and I stopped at nearly every one along the way, topping my gas tank each time. I would take no chances of running out of gas.*

The days were short, being in the dead of winter. The sun was in the southern part of the sky throughout the day, rising in a low arc from east to west, in contrast to the long days of summer when it was directly overhead. By three in the afternoon the shadows had lengthened and it was dark at four o'clock. I was still in the Yukon and determined to make Anchorage that night. But the reality was that it was just too far to go. If I could continue, I would arrive very early in the morning with no place to stay and needing sleep. This wasn't like summer where I could sleep in my car. My finances were limited, having spent a lot of the reserve I had saved for this trip on the transmission. So I plodded on, not feeling as though I could afford to stop and spend the night anywhere.

I had been apprehensive about driving in the dark. The road was not lit and the covering of snow made it difficult to distinguish from the terrain that bordered it. My headlights were the only beacons in this dark terrain, the only light I had to find and follow the road ahead. I was fortunate though that once through Whitehorse and Kluane Lake, there were enough trees and slopes along the highway to make it more visible. I slowly made my way out of the Yukon and crossed the border into Tok, Alaska around seven o'clock in the evening. I had a good ten to twelve hours of driving to go. I kept on. My eyelids began to get heavy and I was fighting sleep. Somewhere around tenthirty I arrived in Glenallen and stopped at a lodge and bar to get a cup of coffee and something to eat.

I sat at the bar and ordered a hamburger and coffee. While I was waiting for it to be served, I nearly fell asleep at my seat. For a moment I actually did, and was awakened by an elderly woman.

"Your food is ready son. Do you want to eat?"

"Yeah, I'm sorry, I'm tired. Been driving all day from Haines."

"Where are you heading?"

"Anchorage. How many hours to get there from here?"

"Ten hours, maybe more at night."

I leaned my head in my hands, rubbed my eyes and started to eat the hamburger in front of me. The women who had been talking to me wandered to another part of the bar and began talking to some of the other customers.

The bar and restaurant were pretty full for a small town out in the middle of the Alaskan tundra. Conversations rose and fell on my ears. This was a typical Alaskan lodge, darkly stained wood decorated with wildlife tapestries and the inanimate heads of moose and caribou overlooking the scene, the bragging rights of the local hunters. Every one of the predators probably had a tall tale attached to a silent gaze from one of the onlooking trophies. A tale of a struggle to the death with the elements and the ultimate triumph of a bullet over the spirit of the wild beast. Even in death these spectators still maintained a dignity all their own, more it seemed than their conquerors, some of whom may have been in the lodge that night, their voices rising above the rest of the room, bragging still on another exploit in life, feeling emboldened, the result of a large volume of alcohol consumed on the first night of the weekend.

I finished my meal and was getting up to leave and pay my bill. I asked for a cup of coffee to go. The woman I had talked to saw me by the door and approached me.

"Son, it's a long way to Anchorage. I know you want to get home but you look too tired to drive anymore"

"Yeah, maybe you're right."

"I own this place. Take this key to cabin number twelve. It's out in the back behind the restaurant. Get some sleep and go in the morning.

"Ma'am, I can't do that. I really don't have enough to pay for it. I don't know where I'm going to be staying in Anchorage yet. I need to save what I have for there."

"Did I say anything about money? I own the place. Now go get some sleep! We serve a good breakfast. I don't want to see you 'til then."

"Thank you, ma'am." I took the key from her and went back to my car and drove around to number twelve. The room was simple enough, a bed, a nightstand, a small chair and table and a separate bath, with a shower. I let my clothes drop where they would and crawled between the sheets of the single bed. It was comfortable and the room was warm. I could hear the wind whistle at times outside, and I was glad to be out of the elements for the moment. I knew that the woman's generosity played in my being here, but I thanked God too for this blessing. He had put me in the right place at the right time with the right generous and kind person. I thought, "Maybe the timing of my return home is ordained. For whatever

reasons, I hadn't been able to make this trip until now. I wondered what she was doing tonight? I hadn't seen her face in seven months. Was she thinking of my return? She knew I was on my way."

As I lay there I tried to picture her. Her long brown hair and large brown eyes. I was still so in love with her. "God, work in her life, bring us together again." I pictured Michelle and Keri, four and two years old, their smiling and happy faces. I could feel their hugs and kisses. I was drifting off to sleep with these thoughts. It would be so good to finally see them after so long. "God, make us a family again." My final thought of the day, like so many other days over the last months. A prayer like so many others.

CHAPTER 38-"LAST LEG"

I woke early the next morning, around five-thirty. The restaurant in the lodge opened at six, so I picked up my Bible and read some. I showered and cleaned up and put on the new clothes I had bought for the trip home. I had shaved and got a haircut about two weeks before and my appearance was a lot different than it was when I left. I looked cleaner, actually pretty "straight", not like I was using drugs, which I hadn't in seven months. Joanne would obviously notice the change, and probably think I've really gone off the deep end with this "religion thing".

I walked outside to take a look around the lodge. I hadn't seen much last night when I came in. It was still dark, but beginning to brighten a bit. I could tell that the sky was clear, which meant cold. As I walked the snow crunched beneath my steps and my hands and face which were exposed to the elements began to numb in just a few short minutes after having left the room. I was not really dressed for the weather and knew if I stayed out much longer my extremities, fingers and nose and ears, would begin to deceptively freeze as frostbite penetrated my skin. I would not feel it at all. The numbing would not be discernible.

I remembered Jack London's description in a short story I had read years ago of a man who died from frostbite in a place similar to where I was. His outside was frozen solid and his inside was still conscious, but his body could not move, and slowly and quietly and agonizingly he expired, unable to do anything to aid himself. I kept moving, kept walking, moved my fingers and rubbed my face. I walked up a row of cabins and back to my room. At the entrance to the lodge was an outside thermometer. It was sixty below zero. I shuddered and went back inside. Even over the short time I had been out I had numbed up and as my skin thawed in the heat from the room, stinging pain shot to the nerve ends in my fingers as they came back to life.

I ate breakfast and sat over a cup of coffee, contemplating the day. Finally I would see my family; I hadn't known on leaving if I ever would again. Here I was not only coming home but with a real hope for reconciliation. "God, be with me today. Help me when I get there. Jesus, I need you."

The lady who owned the place came over to my table and said hello. I thanked her for her hospitality. I hadn't expected it when I arrived last night. She said I looked like I needed sleep, so she just let me get some. I told her a little about my situation and why I was anxious to get to Anchorage yesterday. She wished me the best and headed back towards the kitchen to take care of some of the day's preparations. I paid for breakfast and left a big tip in thanks for the warm bed and rest I had received so graciously at this place.

Heading out toward my car I felt the Lord's presence. It was reassuring. I felt like He was in the timing of my coming back now rather than in January. I didn't know how things would work out, but I had a strong conviction this morning that if I could just stay close to the Lord, they would, and someday my family and I would be under the same roof again. Jesus would do it. Joanne was going to get "saved" someday. I hoped it would be soon. I expected it would as I headed back out to the highway and turned west toward Anchorage and home. I sang a song I had learned at the Friday night Bible study and again felt His nearness as I repeated the words. My heart was stirred and full of the Lord. It was good. Life was good, even with the uncertainty. My state of mind was a long, long way from where it was when I traveled this road going east last summer. I was a changed man. Joanne had heard a lot of talk, now hopefully she would see the walk, the actions to back it up. My appearance would be a shock, but it would have to be more than a new set of clothes and a haircut. She'd have to see Christ in my life. I knew He was there. Would she?

CHAPTER 39-"CLOSE CALL"

Glenallen is in the middle of a vast open area of the mainland of Alaska. It is tundra with relatively flat foothills sloping gently to the south. You could see the southeastern end of the Alaska range toward the north. Ahead, along the horizon, were the slopes of the Chugach range, whose peaks stretched all the way to Anchorage and the Cook Inlet. For now the road was straight and open and the sky was clear. Not a soul was to be seen as I drove along. I was the only one moving it seemed through this vast white wilderness. The sun was a clear orb, settled in its low arc in the southern sky, ascending enough in winter to bring some light, but never really climbing very high. The air was so clear and cold that looking at the sun through the crystalline frost particles, rings could actually be seen around its circumference. They were like daytime northern lights, radiating highlights of color, rainbow-like in appearance. They shimmered in the icy air. If this were night, I thought, I would see a display of northern lights. The conditions were right, clear and cold. The frostbit air clamped the country in its grip.

The highway had been plowed and was nearly clear

*even of packed snow. The Alaskan portion of the
road was paved, which enabled the plows to scrape
the surface when they rolled, which they couldn't do
on the gravel in Canada. It was easier to stay on
the cut of the path here, the black of the tar was
distinct from the surrounding white of the snow piled
on either side and stretching back across the terrain
as far as you could see. The only signs of life were
occasional groups of large black ravens, the vultures
of the northland, on the road ahead of me. I would
chase them away as I drove closer and could see them
lighting again on the black surface in my rearview
mirror after I had passed. I wondered what captured
their attention so on the pavement amidst this vast
dessert of ice and snow.*

*I seemed to be making good time. I would probably
be in Anchorage around two or three in the afternoon.
I would go to see Joanne and the kids first and
leave the Christmas presents I'd been saving for two
months. After that I was planning on going and
finding a church called Abbott Loop Christian Center,
a large congregation I had heard about in Haines. I
needed a place to stay for a night or two and thought
that in a church that size I could hook up with
someone until I got settled. I was counting on their
Christian charity, being a total stranger to them. I
had heard good things about the place and assumed
on their willingness to help. If they didn't, I really
hadn't considered an alternative. I had some money,
but didn't want to spend it on a hotel and sure didn't*

want to stay in downtown Anchorage, which was a rough place, noted for its nighttime population of drunk Eskimos who loved to fight and brawl. I wanted nothing to do with downtown, but I might be forced to go there to find something reasonably priced if I had to.

Around noontime I was ascending a pass over the Chugachs. Sheep Mountain appeared on my right. In the summer you could usually find Dall sheep grazing on its high slopes. Not now. They were completely covered with snow, except for a few outcroppings of blue-gray rock and if they were there, their white coat camouflaged them completely from tourists and predators alike. I passed by the Matanuska glacier which could clearly be seen in the summer. Now its form simply blended with the surrounding white, distinguishable only as large mounds that rose from the flatter profiles of the bordering land at its extremity. The scrub brush and trees that protruded from the snow abruptly ended at the glacier's edge. Beyond was the vast expanse of the icy path rising steadily, like some highway into the heights of the mountain peaks. Its fingers extended through a myriad of valleys and passes into land that had been seen by human eyes but never walked upon by human feet. It was a reminder of an age gone by, when the glaciers carved highways through the earth, piling entire mountain ranges in its wake, the crunched and risen remains of its incredible power.

The higher I got into the mountains the less snow

was on the ground. I wondered why and then felt the car shift slightly as if it was being rocked on its wheels by someone pushing on its side. The wind was howling through the mountain passes where the road cut its course and actually had blown away the snow. There were signs of it higher up toward the peaks and here and there beside the road, but the asphalt itself was clear. It left a strange appearance to the passing terrain. There was a high cloud cover now that hid the sun and removed color from the trees and mountain faces. They looked gray and sullen under the clouds. The trees were bare of leaves. Everything looked stark and grave and ominous with the wind whistling past the car.

The road was bare now and I increased my speed, thinking I could make good time in this stretch. I had forgotten that the appearance of a clear road was deceptive. It was still forty to sixty below and after a bit of travel at forty to fifty miles per hour I hit my first patch of black ice, a frozen patch of sheer ice that reached like a hand across the pavement. I could feel the wheels of the car stop rolling on the frictionless surface and the vehicle slide completely on its own until they grabbed again where the ice ended and the clear road began again. My heart was in my throat and pounding. That out-of-control feeling terrified me. I had slid like that on snow before and sometimes a vehicle will rotate three hundred and sixty degrees, once, maybe even twice, before you can regain control. I quickly slowed down to thirty miles per hour and began to scour the road for signs of the dangerous sheets of ice. They were hard to see, so at every turn I would slow to a crawl in case they were there. Parts of the road were bordered by guard rails that hugged the sides of the mountain's cliff-like faces. A slide at a critical point in a turn could take you over the side. You'd be part of the valley floor after that. Some of the drop-offs had to be four or five hundred feet.

I cautiously made my way along the wind-swept road through the highest parts of the pass. Long stretches, without any of the dangerous ice patches gave me a false sense of security and my speed would climb to forty, forty-five, even fifty miles per hour again. I would catch myself and slow back down to thirty. It wouldn't be long before I began my descent out of the mountains into the Matanuska Valley below, which was the last stretch of my trip before reaching Anchorage. I was anticipating seeing the kids and Joanne with every turn and found myself more often than not, semi-consciously pushing my speed to a dangerous limit.

I had just gone over the height of the pass and was turning to my left to begin a long straight descent down the mountainside. As I turned the horizon spread out before me. I had slowed down considerably to make the turn and as I did I hit a sheet of the dreaded ice. I lost control of the car. It simply drifted through the turn and straight for the side of the road and a drop into what would have been eternity for me. For reasons I'll never know there wasn't any *guardrail along the road at this point, only a short portion on the turn itself, which ended when the road straightened. I was heading for the open portion of the roadside and could do nothing to stop my slide. The guard rail that was there seemed to be behind me and I thought that this was going to be it for me. There was nothing I could do to regain control of the car.*

My eyes opened wide as saucers and I held my breath, just waiting for the car to go over the edge. I thought about trying to open the door and jump out and started to reach for the handle. Suddenly the car lurched somehow from a collision that seemed to come from the right side. The nose of the car moved to the left, and I felt the left front wheel grab the pavement and pull the rest of the car back onto a safe spot free of ice. I slowed down immediately and stopped in the middle of the road. There had been no traffic at all that day, but I wasn't even thinking about that. My foot was trembling as I braked the car and as I opened the door and got out into the frigid cold my knees knocked together violently. I stood in place waiting for my nerves to relax themselves. I couldn't move in any direction, I was shaking so. When my quivering body finally calmed itself, I walked slowly to the edge of the road and peeked over. The drop off down the side of the mountain made me shudder again. My voice broke as I haltingly thanked God for being alive. I looked at the right side of my car and saw a crease on the lower body panels where it had scraped against what must have been the very last portion of guard rail on the turn. A few feet in the wrong direction and nothing would have stopped me from going over the embankment.

The cold began to gnaw at me and I climbed back into the car, which I had left running. Ever so cautiously I crawled away from the spot where, looking back in the rearview mirror, I realized I could have died at. My thoughts were as numb as my jangled nerves. Slowly they began to surface in my mind again. I was so thankful for being alive. I would see my family yet, but for a moment that hope had nearly slid away.

CHAPTER 40-"HOME AT LAST"

Driving across the Matanuska Valley now through Palmer and out towards Anchorage on the last leg of my trip home I thought back to the unexpected stay at the lodge in Glenallen and the brush with catastrophe in the mountains. Clearly it seemed that someone was watching over me. As Anchorage came nearer and nearer, the sense of uncertainty about the future seemed to escalate. I had left this town seven months ago, not knowing if I ever would return. I was back now, a changed person, with a hope in God I didn't have when I left. An inner voice and a sense in my spirit that He would work things out in my marriage, more than anything else, was the reason I had returned. The Bible talks about faith being something that isn't seen with the eyes, something that is hoped for and envisioned in the mind and the soul. Not much substance that people could touch and see, yet a definite force working in my life. The fact that I was here was proof of that. I thought back to the statement I had made to Joanne just before I left, how I would pray to God because He was the only one who could put our marriage back together again. How true that had become in my thinking now. It seemed almost prophetic to have said that, not knowing at the time if there even was a God who cared. I recalled again the episode with the tape player when God seemed to be speaking directly to me about restoring my home. I was living on these ethereal messages and circumstances of hope, on Bible verses and encouragement from people in the church. The days ahead would be another test of the reality of the God I had come to know. How the events would be played out in the theater of our lives was about to be revealed. A new scene and act was about to begin. I was somewhat apprehensive and somewhat confident, a mix of the two. Perhaps that would produce a necessary humility in my attitude toward Joanne. I didn't want to present Jesus to her stridently. I had fallen down in that area in phone conversations already. Now that we were face to face again, how would I handle it? My mind seemed to track along these thoughts continually, keeping pace with the steady motion of the car as it approached its destination at last.

I parked in the area behind the apartments and looked up at the window where Joanne had stood and watched me leave what seemed like an eternity ago. I glanced behind at the bushes where I had lain on my back gazing at a gloomy sky and seemingly hopeless future months ago.

Looking once more at the window I headed toward the door and the stairway to the second-floor apartment. Michelle and Keri were looking back out now. I thought I would melt. My knees felt weak, but seeing them I bounded up the steps, two and three at a time. They opened the door and I bent down to their hugs. My eyes misted with tears of joy. The three of us embraced for a long time, kissing and hugging. I could hear "daddy, daddy" whispered in my ear.

Standing up I looked at Joanne. I realized how much I still loved her in that first look. Her eyes too seemed a little teary, as we looked at each other again after such a long time. It was awkward I wanted so much to embrace her, but couldn't. Her face was always the picture of beauty, the distinctness of her Italian race, her olive skin and deep brown eyes, set in the flows of her raven hair. She canvassed my senses.

"Hello," I finally said.

"Hi."

The kids clung to my legs as we stood and talked in the doorway.

"You got a haircut."

"Yeah, cleaning up my act."

"Come in." Everything looked so familiar, as I remembered it.

"I have some presents in the car from Christmas. Let me go get them. Girls, I'll be right back, got some presents for you."

Michelle followed me out to the car, as if she was

afraid I might leave again for seven months.

"Help me carry these, hon." I gave her a few of the presents Florence had wrapped for me in some other place, some other time, which at the moment seemed very long ago and far away.

Back upstairs Joanne and I spent the next few minutes watching the kids have a second Christmas as we probed each other hesitatingly with our small talk.

"I can't get over your clean-cut look, no beard, no long hair."

"Yeah, a lot has changed as you know."

"Yeah."

"It's great to see them again." I looked down to the floor where they were opening the gifts. Keri still had that sweetness in her face and Michelle still had the strength she always showed in their sibling relationship. She monitored unconsciously the package-opening between her and her sister. It was low key and non-threatening. I smiled as Michelle directed, "This one's yours, this one's mine." Keri didn't mind, as usual, content to have what Michelle allowed her, always so secure in herself and her place, to follow her older sister's lead.

"Where are you staying?" Joanne asked, breaking my reverie of watching the kids.

"I don't really know yet. There's a church in the

area, a big one. I'm sort of hoping to throw myself on them and find a place to land for a few days 'til I find a job and get situated."

"That's not like you," she said, knowing how I didn't like to impose myself on others, how self-reliant I prided myself to be.

"Yeah, it will only be temporary."

We watched the kids finish opening what remained of the presents. I had brought a couple of things for Joanne from Haines. She loved to paint and I bought a small Northern lights reproduction, table-top size. She liked it.

The scene was serene. It was like Christmas again. I thought to myself, "Jesus is here in some way at our first meeting." It was nice sitting together in the living room. To an observer we looked like a happy family, mom and dad and the kids opening Christmas presents.

Joanne put aside the wrappings from the painting. "I got your lovebirds in the mail. I really like them. I cried when I got them. They're nice."

"I knew you would like those." I had seen them in a little shop in Haines, a soapstone sculpture of two tiny birds with their beaks together in what looked like a kiss. They kind of jumped out at me. I remembered again how I felt the Lord had helped me find them. Gifts can say more than words often. That one had.

The late afternoon sun shone through the large picture windows into the room. I had always loved this apartment. We had chosen it because of its view. You could see the entire range of the Chugachs that rimmed Anchorage, from Palmer in the north to the inlet and Turnagain Arm toward the south.

"I've got to go. I've never been to this church, Abbott Loop Christian Center, somewhere up around Huffman and O'Malley. I don't want to get there after dark."

I got up to leave. The kids were preoccupied with the toys I had bought them. They got up and hugged me though as I headed toward the door.

"Daddy will be over to see you real soon. I love you." The three of us embraced again one last time. I looked longingly at Joanne as I turned toward the door.

"Good to see you. I'll let you know my arrangements as soon as I know them myself."

"Okay, bye."

I knew Joanne had talked to them about my not staying with them. It was awkward. Michelle seemed to cling extra hard to my leg as I moved away. She came with me down the stairs to my car. I picked her up and carried her with me, and kissed her hard on the cheek.

"Get back inside, you're going to freeze. I'll be back

to see you in a few days, maybe even tomorrow." She headed back to the door that went upstairs. Joanne and Keri were standing there waiting for her. I walked back to the door and hugged Keri goodbye one last time. One more hug I wanted but couldn't have.

I drove out of the parking area and looked back at the three of them still standing in the doorway. Time seemed to stop for a moment, frozen with everything else inside me, like the cold Artic air between me and them. I wanted to just go back, but had to leave. Finally though I was in Anchorage again. The distance between us was less than it had been for seven months. I took some comfort in that, despite the pain of having to pull away from the apartment. I calmed myself as I drove back out of the complex and headed east toward town.

CHAPTER 41-"ABBOTT LOOP"

I found the Abbott Loop Christian Center without too much trouble. It wasn't far from the apartments. It was about three thirty in the afternoon when I got there.

The church was a large building, but did not have a cohesive design throughout. It had been obviously added to over the years, much of the construction looking fairly new. I could see in the back a new wing was being built. What looked like the original chapel made up the front of the building, with the newer additions growing out of it like the tentacles of an octopus, in every direction the lot would allow. The "Under Construction" sign in the front of the structure seemed a fit description for the present state of affairs.

I parked in a small lot in the front of the building and could see up the hill to the left a large open area where the bulk of the parking must have been. A long temporary stairway brought you down from there to the labyrinth of wings that made up the building below. I walked into an office area, where I noticed some lights on, and asked the first person I saw if I could talk to someone in charge. The man had the look of an office administrator, wearing a white shirt and tie, loosened at the collar and unbuttoned. I thought this was kind of formal attire in Alaska on a Saturday afternoon. He asked me what he could do for me and I told him I had just come into town and was looking for some temporary shelter for a night or two while I found work and a place of my own. He motioned for me to have a seat in what looked like a small waiting area with some straight-backed, uncomfortable chairs. Everything seemed makeshift and temporary in the place, like the personnel in the office were waiting for some new accommodations being built somewhere else on the property. Nothing grand or pretentious about the offices I could see from the waiting area. If anything they were functional, which seemed to be the driving force behind all the architecture I had seen so far. I could hear the man talking to someone quietly from some office down a way from where I sat and soon he returned with another man, who extended a hand of greeting to me.

"Hi, I'm Mike Premo. I'm an evangelist here. This is Curtis Litton, one of our pastors."

I reached out my hand to a guy probably my age, with a thick crop of curly blond hair that looked as though it had recently been cut. He had the look of an "ex-long hair" and I imagined with his thick, tight curls that at one time he sported a pretty large "afro". He had a strong voice which projected itself throughout the office and carried in its tone an air of confidence and self-assurance. A thin, wispy mustache could barely be seen on his upper lip, another sign of what I thought revealed his former lifestyle. We had a kind of immediate unspoken rapport, an understanding, as I was sure he could see through my recent semi-cleaned up appearance, the signs of our similar backgrounds.

"I'm Carl Gove, nice to meet you."

I shook hands with Mike and Curtis. Curtis quietly headed back to the office area leaving Mike and I. We sat down in a couple of the chairs in the waiting room.

"Well, how can we help you?"

"I've just come in from Haines, down near Juneau. I used to live here. I heard about your church from some people there. My wife and I were separated seven months ago. I ended up down there where I got saved. I'm back here hoping the Lord will reconcile my marriage. I've got two daughters here too. I'm a carpenter. I frame houses. I've worked here for two and a half years in the trade. Know a lot of contractors and framers. I need a place to stay for a couple of nights until I get situated. I'll be looking for work on Monday morning."

I said alot, but I felt comfortable to do that with him. I hoped I wouldn't come across as a "freeloader". Apparently I didn't.

"Wait here. We have a Bible college and some of the students stay at homes of people who go to church. I'll see if there's an open bed somewhere in one of the *houses."*

"Okay, thanks Mike."

He headed back toward the offices and I sat back down in the chair. I realized that I hadn't given much thought to where I would stay when I got here. I had somehow assumed on the hospitality of this church, from what I had heard of it in Haines. Some people had passed through on their way from Anchorage and had told me about Abbott Loop at the Friday night Bible study. I didn't really have an alternate plan if this didn't work out. I had been so preoccupied with my car repairs and just getting here. I figured I would be able to find work, even though it was mid-winter and jobs would be at a minimum until the spring thaw. I had never had any problems in previous winters.

Mike was back shortly. "Found a place out here by O'Malley Road where they have a bed. I'll drive you out there and introduce you, you can follow me in your car.

"Great, thanks again."

We headed back out toward the main door.

"Let me show you the church before we leave."

We took a right turn down an aisleway which opened up on a very large sanctuary area. It was late afternoon and beginning to get dark, but I could still make out most of the details of the room, which was still lit by the remaining daylight coming through a row of high windows which lined the west wall. Row upon row of pews stretched in three large sections across and up to the back wall, where three sets of double doors opened into a lobby. We were standing on the side of a large raised platform area in the front. A hand rail about waist height stretched across the front of this stage, with a kneeling ledge along the length of the floor, similar to the one in my tiny church in Haines. Comfortable again for prayer and I assumed this was what it was for, where people could come and pray. There was an open area, ten or twelve feet wide, between this kneeling ledge and the first row of pews. A simple wooden pulpit stood at center stage and behind it and radiating circularly around it, some folding chairs were arranged in rows. This looked like an orchestra section. Further back, at the rear of the stage were some bleacher seats which probably were used for a choir.

"We can seat almost twelve hundred in here," Mike said "We normally run eight hundred to a thousand, more on Sunday mornings. We have a big orchestra which we 'praise the Lord' with and a choir. It's a cool church. You'll like it."

"I'm sure I will. I haven't been in a church this big since I was a kid, but ours looked more like a cathedral. I don't see any stained-glass here."

"No, this just kind of works. God is moving here. You'll see tomorrow. Service is at ten o'clock, we have

Sunday school at nine and prayer in the old chapel at eight thirty. There's another service at six. I'm preaching at that one. Dick Benjamin, the "founding father" of this place, is preaching in the morning. Like I said, you'll like it, we'll keep you busy tomorrow."

"Yeah, that will be good I'm looking forward to it."

"Let's get going. We probably have time to get you there before they eat. You're probably hungry, huh?"

"Yeah, I got in about two and went over to see the wife and kids. That was pretty emotional after seven months. Then I came here."

"By the way, there's a guy named Harold House I'll introduce you to tomorrow. He's in charge of all the new construction around here. He may be able to use you on his crew."

"Man, this is something. That would be great."

We headed out to the cars. I followed Mike back to the main highway which ran north and south through town. We drove up O'Malley Road, one of a number of roads that ran up from the highway into the foothills of the Chugachs which ran along the entire east side of Anchorage. We must have gone about three miles from the church when we pulled into the driveway of a large ranch style home along O'Malley.

CHAPTER 42-"HOSPITALITY"

Mike introduced me to the matron of the house, her name was Betty Stevenson. This woman embraced chaos, somehow finding an order and purpose for herself in the midst of it. The house seemed to have been converted into a dormitory for young male Bible college students. The rooms were crowded with bunkbeds and cots and there seemed to be little area in the entire house left for just living. Her husband wasn't there at the time and I wondered if he even felt comfortable in his home when it was like this. I took an upper berth in a bunkbed in one of the bedrooms. From adjoining rooms I could hear the constant hum of conversation. I wondered if I would get any sleep tonight and how would I ever get into a bathroom in the morning.

Betty was a very hospitable lady, outgoing, friendly, genuinely caring in the comments she made as I related my situation to her. I had arrived in time to join everyone for a dish of spaghetti and some garlic bread. She made me a cup of coffee and we just talked for a while. I was unwinding from the long trip and soon felt tired. I told her I was just going to go to bed early and would set an alarm to try and beat the crowd in the morning before church. I wanted to take in the full menu of events. I would try and be there for the prayer time at eight thirty and then the Sunday school. I was looking forward to it all. I thought how the Lord seemed to continue to be making a way for me in coming back. I had a place to stay, had seemingly found a church, and possibly even a job.

I cleaned up after dinner and propped myself in the bunk with my Bible, wanting to read a bit before going to bed. People were coming and going in and out. I believe we had five beds in the room. It was really crowded. Almost reminded me of the commune I had slept at years ago back in Massachusetts, but this was an entirely different place than that. In spite of the hectivity, there was a sense of order and direction and a good feeling about it. It hadn't taken long to notice that. People were excited about life here. They were up. Different guys would come into the room and say hello to me and talk for a moment. They were sympathetic with my condition and offered to pray with me for my family. They were all excited about the church. Apparently many people were coming to the Lord during the services and a sense of God's presence could be felt at the meetings.

They esteemed Dick Benjamin, the lead pastor, highly. He was respected, as was Mike. Mike had done a lot of work in the area and all over Alaska with a rock group which took music and the Jesus message wherever they could go and do concerts. A lot of people were coming into the church through *his evangelistic efforts. The church had opened their arms to the "long-hairs", who, like me, had flocked to the north country in droves, looking for peace and work away from the trappings of urban America. We had brought our drugs and hang-ups with us and many had come to places of disillusionment when we found that a beautiful surrounding still wasn't enough to give us what we were searching for. Like me, many had come to the Lord, where we found real peace, what we longed for. This church, like few others, had opened themselves to accept us. They had let down their guard and loosened their shirt collars, so to speak, and their numbers had swelled, from a group of thirty, meeting in an old Quonset hut to what I had seen that day, a place that seated a thousand. It wasn't easy accepting "hippies" and was apparently painful for some of the older members. Change can be that way, but they were led by a strong man, Dick Benjamin, who had stretched himself.*

Dick and Mike were chief architects in the transition. Mike, the converted long-hair, convinced Dick that "hippies" would respond to the Gospel if someone would reach out to them. Dick had been willing to change and do that, and the results were immediate. Apparently they had been growing ever since. I looked forward to hearing both of them speak the next day. The conversations with the sold-out Bible school students had communicated to me the excitement that was a part of the church. I could see it in Betty too. This was going to be a much different church experience than Haines, I could tell already. I thought back to all my friends there and could picture Don in the pulpit the next day. The distance seemed greater than the eight hundred miles I had traveled. I was out of the incubator of my life with the Lord. Everything was new and different now and my being back would intensify the whole situation with Joanne. It would be trial by fire from here on out. I had my faith that God would bring us back together, but I didn't have a clue how and I sensed tonight it would be a struggle for all of us, for Joanne, me and the kids too.

CHAPTER 43-"CHURCH"

I was up early in the morning and managed a shower before the troops arrived in the bathroom. I don't know how they did it here. They must have added extra bathrooms in the house I thought. How else could they survive with so many people?

I drove back along the highway to the church and parked this time in the upper lot. I walked down the long wooden stair and through a building that was still being worked on inside. It looked like new classrooms for a school which was part of the church too.

I made my way to what was the original chapel where they had prayer meetings before all of the services. There were so many people there. They weren't shy about their praying. They talked aloud to the Lord without embarrassment. I was a little uncomfortable at first. We didn't pray that way in Haines. But not everyone was loud. Some knelt quietly with their eyes closed, others stood with their hands raised toward heaven. All of the styles seemed to mingle together in what sounded like a symphony of prayer rising from the room to the Lord. It moved me. I knelt along an altar rail at the front of the room and bowed my head and just listened for a moment. Different people came behind me and laid hands on my shoulders. I could hear them praying for me. It was comforting. I recognized Mike's voice praying.

At nine o'clock everyone headed into the sanctuary for the Sunday school class. I took a seat in the middle of the large auditorium and saw a balding, authoritative looking man approach the platform. He hooked up to the sound system and began his Bible study. I learned from a printed handout that this was Dick Strutz, a teacher in the congregation and one of the staff. Apparently there were a great number of assistant pastors and teachers and counselors at the church. With a congregation of so many, they were needed

The Bible study was on "faith", believing God for things that we didn't yet see in reality, but hoped for. It related so well to where I was at with my family. I had a great sense of being in the right place here at the church. When the study was over, I felt lifted up, as if God had again spoken to me personally to continue to believe for the reconciling of my marriage. After the class I took a seat closer to the front, only about three rows back from the first.

People began to fill the room now. Just prior to ten I looked around and the place was practically full. There was a steady stream of conversation, all centered around the Lord. There was definitely an excitement in the air, almost as if everyone anticipated some great event that was about to take place. The church seemed to be predominately young, people that looked to be around my age, but older people and children were not scarce in numbers by any means. It was a real cross section of humanity, from young to old and everything in between.

A couple sat down next to me in the pew. They were older, she was tall and thin. A pretty face with tightly pursed lips and large deep brown eyes. She smiled at me as she took her seat. Her husband had a crown of thick black hair, with no signs of graying, though his forehead and cheeks were wrinkled with the beginnings of older age. His complexion was ruddy and weathered looking, like many of the men of the north, a feature worn into the face by the severity of the many winters of working outside. His hands were those of a tradesman.

Musicians were taking their places around the stage and the choir ordered themselves on the steps of the bleacher seats. There were two pianos to the left of the stage I hadn't noticed in the dim light of the room yesterday afternoon. Guitar players, flutes, trumpets, saxes, it was an informal gathering of sounds that looked more as if they would be played extempore than from a rigid practice session during the week.

A young man took his place behind the pulpit, greeted everyone warmly, said a short prayer and then asked everybody to stand and sing. An overhead *screen was lowered as he spoke and the words of the first song appeared on the textured surface, large enough to be visible even from the back of the church. The room swelled with the sounds of the orchestra and when twelve hundred people began to sing I had to just look around from my seat in the front. People were full of emotion, some smiling, some with their eyes closed, some clapping, others with hands raised. Everyone was involved expressing through the music their love for God. They seemed to be singing directly to Him, not to each other or for the song leader. I remembered some of the times when we would sing at the Friday night Bible study in Haines. This reminded me of that, but on a much larger scale. With the upbeat song there was an atmosphere of celebration and joy.*

I was overwhelmed with emotion at the sight of so many people focusing on the Lord. I began to weep and turned back to the front and bowed my head, sobbing almost convulsively. I tried to control, as best I could, the heaving I felt in my chest. I could hear the sounds of the singing filling the entire auditorium. It was like a great choir lifting its voices in a wonderful spontaneity to a single source. There were simultaneously commingled expressions of love and thanksgiving and deep appreciation to a person that couldn't be seen, but already seemed to be felt in the meeting. Jesus' Spirit seemed to be there. The lady sitting next to me placed her hand lightly on my shoulder as I sobbed. She seemed to sense without spoken words the awe I was feeling at the moment. I gained control of my weeping and began to sing.

For the next half an hour we went from one song to the next in a continual flow of praise to God. The first few songs were hand clappers, then the tempo slowed and "songs of the heart" were sung with a reverence I had never seen in a church prior to this day. I closed my eyes as I sang, expressing myself to the One who had changed me and given me hope. I could picture Joanne and the kids and at times my singing seemed to be a prayer in song. Scriptures were put to music that lifted me and built my faith in the outcome of our struggle. He was there, you could sense it. The air seemed thick with His presence, something almost tangible that you could definitely feel. As if in response to the symphony of praise, He showed up, the honored guest to whom this service was directed.

Dick Benjamin preached. When his sermon ended, there was an extended altar call for people who wanted to give their life to the Lord or be "baptized in the Holy Spirit". There was some response and those who came forward to the front of the church were escorted to a private place outside the sanctuary by another one of the ministers on staff. I noticed that Mike, apparently because he was the church evangelist, went with the ones who wanted to be "saved" that day. Harold House and his wife were introduced as the people who would pray with those who wanted to be "Spirit-filled". I remembered he was the one Mike had mentioned who ran the work crews *on the buildings. I thought to myself that I would talk to him maybe that night about a job, as I watched he and his wife leave the room with maybe a group of eight or ten people.*

Dick Benjamin then called for the remaining ministers and "elders" to come to the stage. They lined up across the entire raised portion of the front platform, a group of almost thirty men, all dressed well, every one of them clean-shaven and wearing a tie. It was impressive, though slightly intimidating, to see them there. The "elders" were layman who assisted in the administration and ministry of the church. They looked to be generally older men. I eventually learned that they were not paid staff, but volunteered and were chosen to serve because of their solid place in the church and reputation in the community.

An invitation was given to "any and all" to come forward to the altar and seek out one of the men for prayer for anything you had need of. People in the congregation responded and descended on the open area in front of the stage like a flood. Those who had prayer requests went to particular ones or simply kneeled at the altar rails. Many were not there to be prayed for but to pray for a friend or family member or even someone they didn't know but just felt impressed to lend their support. The men on the stage were the overseers of the scene that unfolded. The quiet hum of prayer ascended from the place. Those who didn't come forward mingled in the auditorium, visiting, but in respectful ways, aware of what was happening at the front of the church. Some began to make their way out the back, heading for home and the remains of the day.

I watched for a moment and then made my way through the crowd, to the rail in front of the stage. I felt the press of many people around me as I asked one of the men for prayer for my family. Others there listened as I briefly explained my situation. I told them I intended to go from here to visit them that afternoon. As I bowed my head, hands were placed on my shoulders it seemed from everywhere. It gave me a tremendous sense of comfort and was almost like a covering from the arrows of life that sometime penetrated our experience with their pain and testing. I could hear prayers being spoken, one elders' voice rising above the rest in an eloquent prayer for restoration in my home. My eyes moistened slightly with tears. I hardly wanted it to end. I felt safe in the arms of His love being fleshed out by His people that morning, people that didn't know me but they seemed to be bonding with me already. They were sharing my grief and my hope together. "This church stuff is good stuff," I thought to myself. A lot of real support being expressed here. It lifted me.

The prayers rose to a zenith of emotion and then began to recede. When I had that sense that they were pretty much over, I raised my head and turned to leave. I smiled at those around me, thanking them with my eyes and made my way through the crowded area back to my seat, listening as I went to the activity of so many praying. I hadn't seen this many people involved like this ever in a church before. It seemed so natural and so supportive, like something we were supposed to do often.

The couple I sat next to were waiting for me when I got to my seat. They introduced themselves and asked me if my wife's name was Joanne.

"Yes," I said with some surprise, "Do you know her?"

"We think so, we heard you mention she lived out on Jewel Lake Road. Our son is going out with a lady who lives in the apartment underneath her. You have two little daughters, don't you."

"Yes, that's her." I was amazed at this coincidence. "Stan is your son? You're talking about Donna, his girlfriend, aren't you?"

"That's her." We smiled at each other. "We've heard about you. You were away a while weren't you?"

"Yes, I just got back here yesterday. I was in Haines working. I got saved there and now I'm back, hoping the Lord will heal my marriage."

"Well, this isn't an accident, our sitting next to you. We've been praying for Stan. He needs the Lord too. We'll have you over our house sometime for dinner."

"That would be great. What a coincidence, or probably not. Nice meeting you."

We said goodbye and they turned to leave. I sat back down in my seat and marveled at what seemed to me to be God's providence in my affairs. I didn't know how things would go from here on out, but I was increasingly realizing that maybe He did after all. Maybe I could let go a bit and trust Him and the results would be what I was hoping for. I had tried to stage and control so much up to this point. Maybe I could back off and let someone greater take control. I quietly meditated on all this as I sat there in the church. People were still at the front, now a half-hour after the service. Some of the men who had been up front were in deep conversation with individuals or couples, leaning over the stage to listen, or sitting in the pews across the first row. It looked as if some would be there quite a while. I got up and left the sanctuary slowly. Church had been an event for me this morning. I already looked forward to tonight.

CHAPTER 44-"THE DIVIDING LINE"

Time passed. I had worked with Harold House at the church for the remainder of the winter. Alaska's muddy spring had now turned into summer. I had no trouble finding framing work. With the Alaska pipeline being built from the North Slope to Valdez at the head of the Gulf of Alaska, work was plentiful. Houses were being built everywhere to accommodate the oil industry personnel soon to move into Anchorage. Prospects for other pipelines, both oil and natural gas, brought people north in droves to the Last Frontier. I had moved into a house close by Joanne, in the Jewel Lake area, with two roommates from Abbott Loop, "Fred" Westrom and Bruce Donnelly. Fred owned the house and had an extra room which he rented to me.

For Joanne and I, that spring and summer, were painful times. We hurt each other. I pushed way too hard trying to convince her to turn to Jesus like I had. She had attended church with a girlfriend one time just to see what it was like. Curious. Didn't return. She had filed for divorce and in July the divorce was official. That was a real test of my faith and hope.

Like a final nail in a coffin, in the natural realm, our marriage and family were, for all effects, dead and buried. The routine of regular child visits at Fred's place and financial support for Joanne were now in place and I reluctantly settled into it, having no choice in the matter. The Lord would have to remarry us now for our family to go on. I still clung to that possibility though.

One afternoon in late summer, Joanne had agreed to come and visit one of the pastors at the church. I had high hopes that he would be able to influence her, but I think she wanted to tell him not to encourage me to wait for her. I'm sure he explained to her that no one in particular was doing that with me, in fact, more people probably didn't want me to get my hopes so high; they were afraid if things didn't work out the way I wanted them to that the disappointment would be too devastating. I knew they cared, but my faith was motivated and my hope, I always felt, came from my relationship with the Lord and what He was telling me in my spirit would happen. It wasn't coming from people or pastors or church leaders per say. Some people believed with me, others were concerned about picking up the pieces if it didn't happen. They all cared and I appreciated both groups.

I got off from work early, knowing Joanne would be at the church. I was there when she left the office and we decided to meet at a small park on the way back to Jewel Lake.

"What did you talk about?"

"Carl, I tried to tell him not to encourage you to think we're going to get back together someday. We've both changed so much."

"I know, but you can change more. I'm hoping you'll meet the Lord like I did."

"I know you are, but I'm not interested."

I changed the subject, "Michelle is pulling away from me lately."

"What do you mean?"

"She goes into a shell when we're together. Won't talk to anyone. Just lies on the couch, doesn't say anything. When she gets that way, nothing I do or say seems to get through to her. All we've been through is getting to her."

Joanne hung her head and I thought she was going to cry. Her words surprised me, "Carl, why can't you be the way you used to be?"

Was she saying it would make a difference, that we could be together again?

"What are you saying?"

"I don't know, it just came out."

I wanted to put my arm around her, but we just sat in silence and looked out across the clearing of trees *we were sitting beside. It was quiet, you could hear the wind blowing softly. I thought to myself, "She seems to be saying we might be together, if I wasn't a Christian. What an irony, the God I want to bring us together right now is standing between us, for the moment keeping us apart. I want her, more than any other person this side of heaven I want her. But I can't ever go back. I'm different. Unless she comes my way, we'll never be together again." That thought sobered me.*

"I can't change back Joanne. A part of me wants to, because I love you so much, but] can't."

We both silently walked back to our cars, said goodbye and drove out to the main road again. I followed her until she turned toward the apartments. I continued on the short distance to my house. The lines were so drawn in this and it seemed that today we both understood that clearly. She might have still felt something for me. It seemed that way. I hadn't seen that in almost a year. But there was a spiritual distance between us that today couldn't be bridged. It would never work unless we were both believers or both unbelievers. The Bible says it is very hard to have a successful relationship if you're mixed, one a believer, one not. It instructs people to avoid those relationships. I understood that now. I sat in a living room chair back at the house and just thought through it all again. The change in my life was so real it was actually coming between us. I emptied the thoughts from my mind. I felt numb. I despaired.

What if she didn't ever come to the Lord? The pain would continue for the kids. Would Keri withdraw from me too. Hope seemed fleeting in that moment, like it and Joanne were leaving for good. I wanted to reach out and take hold of both, but my mental hands seemed leaden. I dragged my tired body into my bedroom and flopped onto the bed. Exhausted, I drifted off to sleep quickly. It seemed a welcome relief for the time to this unresolvable quandary. I hoped "hope" at least would return when I woke. I drifted away from my thoughts, embracing the semi-consciousness of sleep for the night.

CHAPTER 45-"A DREAM"

Somewhere in time she was in a church, I could not tell if it was Abbott Loop, but it was big, with a large sanctuary. She was going forward for an altar call to receive the Lord. Finally, my hope in God had become a reality. My faith had been justified and rewarded. The Lord was not an imaginary being and my dream had not been an excessive extension of my emotional state during the separation. God had proven His reality in our lives. My wife was saved, just as He had promised I could see her, going down the aisle, her head bowed, a tear in her eye.

I dragged my feet over the side of the bed and onto the floor. It was Saturday and I was taking the day off from work. I could relax at home, make some breakfast and do some reading and pray, maybe take a ride downtown later in the day.

I felt better this morning. The memory of our talk in the park yesterday seemed less ominous. I read some from the Bible and knelt by the chair in the living room to pray. My hope had returned. I had sensed that from the moment I got up. Despair had fled in the night with weeping and hope had come again with the new day. I thanked the Lord for renewing me. How many times He had over the months since last summer. It seemed whenever I needed something He was there in some special way. The tape recorder incident in Haines stood out in particular. There were scriptures, innumerable ones that had spoken to me personally again and again. He would do it. I prayed for her with confidence and began thanking Him for her salvation.

I usually didn't remember dreams. As soon as I would wake I would normally forget them. I had forgotten this one until this moment, kneeling in prayer. Suddenly I could see her again in that church going to an altar to ask Jesus into her life. As I saw this picture in my mind, it was as if I was back asleep. I saw it again exactly as I had drempt it the night before. I opened my eyes to be sure I was awake. There was the living room, the furniture, everything was in its place. The sun was streaming through the window of the sliding class door, through the dining room and into the front room, coloring objects as it made its way across floors and up the walls. The vision had come and gone. I knew it was a replay of the dream. I thought about it, "How unusual for me to be seeing it again. I rarely ever remember a dream."

My conclusion was that this must have come from the Lord, an answer to my prayer for renewed hope drempt out as I slept in the night. God was encouraging me again, speaking to me, sustaining my hope, as He had been doing continually when I needed it the most. He wanted me to hold on, He wanted me *to believe for her. All this set the day moving in a direction that was so totally opposite from the despair I went to bed with. In my final moments of prayer, I thanked Him again for my wife and my new life with Him that was teaching me so thoroughly of a reality in a relationship with God that is not seen or heard yet is just as real as the reality of our physical senses.*

CHAPTER 46-"HEARTBREAK"

The situation with Michelle just kept getting worse. When we were together, she seemed not to want to be with me. I had no idea what to do. I tried everything I knew to reach her, to bring her back to me, but nothing worked.

I had gone to her kindergarten class one day in the afternoon. It was in an elementary school that was close to the apartments. I had driven over there for no real reason. I left work early and had some time to kill before anyone got home at the house, so I stopped by there to see her.

The office people in the school were a little skeptical of my being there. I thought they suspected me of wanting to kidnap her or something. I told them I just wanted to see where she went to school. They said they thought it would be okay if I went into the class for a moment, the kids were on a recess break and I wouldn't be disturbing anything. I followed one of the secretaries back to the classroom.

Michelle was playing in a sandbox, toward the back of the room by herself. I waved to her. She saw me but lowered her head and wouldn't look up. I called to her and she still wouldn't look, she seemed to turn her back to me even. I watched her for a few more moments, but she still didn't budge. I think the teacher and office worker could feel my hurt. It was awkward for them I was sure.

I stood there in stunned silence for another minute or two. Michelle continued to play by herself in the sandbox, ignoring me completely. She didn't want to see me, she didn't want me around

I blurted a muffled "thank you" to the teacher and aide and walked out of the room and back to my car. I drove slowly from the parking lot and headed for home. I was in a daze, numb. I turned down a gravel side street which dead ended in an area of brush and small trees. I could see Joanne's apartment through them across a distance to my right. I remembered once again laying on the ground in another part of this same cluster of brush contemplating ending my life. I was a long way from there, but this situation with Michelle was almost as painful as that was at the time. It was one thing to be estranged from my wife, but to be shunned by my own daughter. This I never expected.

Not thinking I pulled into the brush and stopped. Gripping the wheel as hard as I could I leaned my head forward, resting it, though, at the same time, wanting to bang it against the steering wheel. I may have, I can't remember. I kept saying to myself over and over again, "God is going to restore my home,

God is going to restore my home." I was repeating the expression dumbly, monotonously, not so much because I believed it so strongly at that moment, it was a feeble attempt to try and hold on to something, anything, that would keep me from going over the edge emotionally.

I don't recall how I even got back to the house that night, or going to sleep. I woke up the next day with my clothes still on. The blankets hadn't even been turned down. I slept on top of the bed, probably falling there after making my way home, emotionally exhausted.

I dragged myself to work and pounded nails extra hard that morning, trying to work with an intensity that would somehow relieve some of the pain inside and take my mind off of the events of yesterday afternoon. Jim, my boss, who I had been working with that summer, could tell something had happened and kind of left me to myself and my nail-pounding therapy.

CHAPTER 47-"HURT ON HURT"

I left Fred's house shortly thereafter. Dave and Linda Stewart and their two children, a couple who had recently moved from the lower forty-eight and were living in a trailer parked on Fred's property, needed my room and a friend from church had offered me a room in his place on the other side of town. It was further away from the apartments but I thought that maybe that would be better for me for awhile.

Vince, my new roommate, was single and a few years younger than me. He was an up and optimistic kind of person and told me he had heard about my situation and always felt an intense desire to see my marriage restored. The first night I was there we talked about it extensively. I told him that I sometimes had a tendency to dwell on the situation to a fault. I tried to explain how tied up my life was in it all. He seemed to understand.

He had a couple of other roommates in the apartment and the atmosphere was kind of like a college dormitory. We spent a lot of late nights talking about the Bible and the "things of God", very heady stuff. It was good for me though, took my mind off of the family. At Fred's we didn't see each other as regularly as I saw Vince. Over there, it seemed that Fred and Bruce and I were always coming and going to and from various places and events, so we didn't make as much contact. I stayed at home more at Vince's and got to know him well.

The fall was brilliant, though it quickly waned, as it always does in Anchorage. The early signs of winter were upon us now. The snow line was falling on the mountain peaks again, down into the valleys below, where the temperature was steadily dropping each day. The days were shorter too. I was still seeing the girls every other weekend. We were really cramped in the apartment, but we made due. Vince was accommodating when they were there. This guy was genuine and growing on me. He was unselfish without having to work at it. It came from him in a natural sort of way. A great trait.

I had been with the girls one weekend and late on a Sunday afternoon was getting ready to drive across town and bring them home. It was already dark outside. It had been a tough weekend. Michelle was completely withdrawn. On Saturday we had been over at the church during the day and she lay on a pew and wouldn't talk to anyone. It took two hours before she even slightly got out of her depression. Keri was okay, she would talk and play in a normal way and interacted with me as always. When it was time to take them home, Michelle began to withdraw again.

The ride back to the apartment was quiet. I

would try to get Michelle into a conversation, but she wouldn't have it and sat silently against the passenger door, staring out the window. We drove into the apartment in the gathering gloom of dusk. It's how I felt inside at the moment.

"Give me a kiss goodbye, hon." Michelle just opened the door and headed to the stairway and upstairs.

Keri was still in the car. I pulled her to me and hugged her as once again tears welled up in my eyes. I kissed her goodbye and she got out of the car and headed inside. She looked back at me and smiled. There was nothing as sweet as Keri's smile. It lit up the world.

She had the door to the stairwell opened and then turned and came back toward the car. I leaned over and opened the passenger door again and she climbed back into the front seat, slid over to my side and put her arms around my neck.

"I love you daddy. It's going to be all right."

Tears flowed down my cheeks like a river now. I held onto her, not wanting to let go. How a three-year-old could have the capacity to feel my pain was beyond me.

"You'd better go upstairs. Mommy is probably waiting for you. I love you. You're such a good girl."

I kissed her on the cheek and watched as she went inside. I smiled at her when she looked back one last time. What a gift she was. No one could have done more than she had at that moment. I still couldn't understand it. I drove away thinking about it. It seems that the Lord graces our lives at times when we least expect it, prompting a three-year-old little girl to come back to comfort her hurting father. There was nothing intellectual about it. She simply had an inclination and with childlike innocence responded to it. I would never forget this.

CHAPTER 48-"RESIGNATION"

I left work early the next day and drove over to the church. I wanted to talk to Jim Brenn. Dick Benjamin was out of town and Jim kind of manned the ship while he was gone. I had developed a close relationship with him over the months Jim had been at the church. He was the one who had talked to Joanne when she came by the church a couple of months before.

I hadn't made an appointment, but Jim made a spot on his schedule to see me. I sat down across from him in his office. He always opened any time he spent with people in prayer, so together we bowed our heads and asked the Lord to join us.

"What going on, Carl?"

"Things are getting pretty bad with Joanne and now with the kids. Michelle has withdrawn from me. She's really taking all of this pretty hard. Four years old. It's sad. She barely speaks to me when we're together. Just sits by herself or lays down on a couch or chair. You can't reach her. She has such a forlorn look on her face. It's killing me to see this. Losing Joanne has been tough enough, seeing her pull away though..., now I

feel like I'm losing my children. I don't think I can keep a real meaningful relationship going with them with just every other weekend. I don't know what to do sometimes."

"What have you been thinking about?"

"I feel like my being around is just causing hurt right now for everyone, for Joanne and the kids. I'm hurting too. Maybe I should not see them for awhile. It goes against my grain, but I don't want to continue to be a source of nothing but hurt in their lives. Sometimes that's the way it seems."

"There would be nothing wrong with that, Carl."

"I still want my marriage restored. I'm still believing the Lord for that. but I need to get on with my life until that happens. I'm living in rooms in other people's houses. I need a place of my own. Somewhere I can go home to at night, maybe learn to cook, that would be something, have a room for the kids when they visit, my own mailbox, something like a real home. Backing off from seeing them seems in my mind to be giving up a bit. But I need a rest and so do they. I feel like it's the right thing to do right now. It would just be temporary, while I get settled in a place. I might call Joanne and tell her this week. What do you think? Am I giving up. Am I doubting God, resigning myself to not getting back together with Joanne?"

"You know in your heart that that could never

happen. That's not what I'm hearing. Carl, you're tired. I've watched you, been around you, have seen you carry this for as long as I've known you. People here care about you. You've been faithful to your marriage. I admire you for that. But I see you hurting too, and I hurt with you. I want you to take a break from your family for say a month. Draw close to the Lord and see what He's saying to you. I don't suspect it will be any different than what you've heard from Him in the past, but I sense you need a break, need some time alone with Him and with your church to regroup. It hurts us all to see you hurt. Heal up emotionally for a time and gather some strength. I think it's right on for you to get your own place and make a home for whoever is going to be there. As your pastor, I say to do it, take a break, for however long is right and reasonable to build yourself up again. You guys are all beaten down by all the emotion of this. It might happen this way all over again in the future, but for now, give yourself and them a rest."

"Yeah, that's kind of how I feel. I'm coming apart under all the strain and they are too."

"All right, do it for awhile. Let me pray with you."

We prayed together. I barely heard what Jim prayed. I kept feeling on the one hand like this was the thing to do, but on the other that I was giving up, not pressing ahead toward what I believed the Lord wanted to do. I was tom, but I got up to leave with a resolve to stay away for at least a few weeks and see where I was at. Jim said we could talk again at that time.

I left the office and headed down the hallway toward the front door. I passed Tom Edmunson's office, one of the men on staff at the church. His door was ajar and when he saw me, he asked me to come in.

"How are you?" He asked this with such an air of spiritual authority. He could talk, asking a very natural question like that, and put the fear of God in a man. He was powerful and persuasive. He could rivet a moment in time.

"I just got done talking wth Jim. Things have been going downhill with Joanne and now the kids are pulling away from me. I've pretty much decided to go on with my life for a time and if God is going to restore my home, he doesn't need me around to do it."

I had come a long way from Haines, where I used to try and persuade Joanne about the claims of the Gospel. I never argued with her about Jesus or the Bible anymore. When the divorce came through I let go a little more. Now circumstances were forcing me even further from their lives. I thought that this was really in God's hands now. Maybe that's what He wanted all along.

I drifted back from my musing when I heard Tom say, "Wait here a moment, I'll be right back."

I didn't know what this was about, but he had a serious tone in his voice as he got up and left the room.

A few moments later he was back with a handkerchief and a small bottle of oil. These weren't weird religious articles, as you might think, but we used them in praying for people, because the practice had a basis in scripture. Paul the apostle used to pray for people who weren't physically present by laying his hands on a handkerchief and praying. It was a point of contact. The Bible says people were healed and delivered when he did this, even though they weren't in his presence. Using oil to anoint people for prayer is both an Old and New Testament practice. We simply would place a small drop on the forehead before we prayed. It was a symbol of the anointing of the Holy Spirit and of our faith and hope that the Lord would come and minister to the person according to our requests.

Tom opened the bottle of oil and sprinkled a few drops on the handkerchief. Another pastor, Curtis Litton, who I had met with Mike the day I arrived at Abbott Loop, had stepped into the entrance of Tom's open door and Tom, looking up, asked him to join us as we prayed.

"Curtis, come on in. You know Carl. We're going to pray for him and his family. He's going through it and I felt prompted to get this handkerchief and anoint it and pray for his wife. You can join us."

We gathered around the prayer cloth and Tom began. "Satan, in the name of Jesus we take authority over you and over the darkness that surrounds Joanne. We bind you and break your power and we call on the Holy Spirit of God to come in like a mighty wind into the place you have vacated and minister to Joanne and cause her to come to Jesus Christ. We speak not in our own authority but in the authority of Jesus Christ, our risen Lord. Amen!"

That was Tom Edmunson. Decisive and powerful. He sensed God's voice speaking to Him, which prompted him this late afternoon to do what he had just done. He was humble and unpretentious, but with a recognized authority in his life that could only have come from his relationship with Jesus. I was moved by the prayer he had just spoken and walked out of the office with hope renewed again. Before I even could get out of the church office, the Lord had shown me that He wanted me to still hold on to the promise of reconciliation; I had moments before told Jim Brenn basically that I would back off and listen for the Lord to confirm again His promise to me concerning my family. Immediately now, He had begun to do that. I hadn't even got out to the parking lot and my car.

I drove home thinking long and hard on that fact. I talked to Vince about it. I concluded that nothing had changed, God had spoken to me again through Tom's prayer and prompting that I was to continue to believe and hope for Joanne to come to know Jesus. For a moment, I had let go of it all today and had only picked it up again because the Lord showed me clearly that He wanted me to. He would do the work and He wanted me to continue to believe that and look to Him as He led me through this.

Vince seemed to agree with me. "I don't think the Lord wants you to carry it as much, He wants to carry this load for you Carl, but He still wants you to hope for restoration. Sounds contradictory I know, but it makes sense to me. Can you see what I mean?"

"Yeah, it's kind of a let go but don't let go at the same time. I guess even if I don't see them as much in the near term, the Lord still wants me to hope and pray. I think I can do that better now than I ever could have in the past. We'll see."

CHAPTER 49-"A TEACHING MOMENT"

Two weeks after my meeting with Jim Brenn, I went to church on Sunday morning. This was to have been my scheduled weekend to see the girls and I had called Joanne to tell her I wouldn't be coming and the reason why. She agreed it might be a good thing for the time being. I said it would only be temporary and she seemed glad for that. I had talked to both Michelle and Keri on the phone, but made no mention of my intentions to them. They probably really wouldn't notice if I didn't come one weekend. I felt unsettled about not seeing them. It had become a regular activity for us for quite some time now.

I was feeling a little low during the service and when it was over, I lingered in the main sanctuary for some time, watching the people being prayed for at the front. I was having a broken conversation with the Lord in my seat, broken by my own train of thoughts about Joanne, the kids, the whole situation. It had been a long ordeal, the separation, the divorce. I had come such a long way from where I was. There had been low points since then, but I had never reached complete despair. There was always continued hope since meeting the Lord. He was always there to boost me in some way when I got down. I was still convinced that He would bring us back together, but over the course of the last year, I had imagined all kinds of ways that it would happen. I was seemingly at the end of trying to figure out how He would accomplish it anymore. Whatever He did would be His plan. I felt like I was out of the way in terms of trying to help Him out. Maybe that's where He had wanted me all along. I had been broken by the circumstances that had developed through all this to the point where I was now. I had a hope for reconciliation, but perhaps finally I had given the means to that end over to the Lord. I was nearly out of the picture now with Joanne and even the kids. I knew I would see them again, but I didn't know for sure how soon.

I came back to my surroundings from the place of my meditation and the church was practically empty. A few of the elders were still scattered about the auditorium in conversation with different individuals, probably concerning some issue in their lives. I wanted to stick around a while longer and pray some more, just have some quiet time with the Lord. I thought I would leave the sanctuary and go to the prayer room which was close by.

I went in and went to the front where an altar rail stretched across the width of the room. I knelt there and bowed my head and actually fell asleep with my head on my hands.

I don't know how long I slept, but when I woke, I knew that it was afternoon now, maybe two o'clock. I could hear no sounds from anywhere else in the church. I may have been the only one in the building.

I continued to kneel quietly at the altar, not thinking or even praying. My thoughts for the moment seemed to have stopped their endless flow. The windows of the room were of stained glass, which softened the bright light of the sunny day shining through them onto the side walls. It was very quiet there, peaceful, you could have heard a pin drop.

Thoughts of Joanne began to come back to my mind. I could almost picture her in the quiet softness of the chapel. Nothing of my love for her had diminished through all the hurt and pain we had both endured. I had my Bible with me and opened it to the book of 1st Corinthians. I wanted to read the "love" chapter, chapter 13. It describes God's love. I wanted to see my love for Joanne in the verses. I wanted my love for her to be like that. I wanted to see a comparison as I read the verses. Ha! I read, "Love is patient, love is kind. love does not behave itself unseemly, does not seek its own way." "Does not seek its own way". I read the words again and then once again. I was stuck on them. I began thinking about my love for Joanne. In the light of the words I had read, I thought that my love for her was certainly not like that. It seemed that everything I did in relationship to her, to try and reach her, to try and persuade her to believe in Jesus, had a mixed motive. Yes, I wanted her to know the Lord, to get saved, but I knew that if that happened it would hopefully mean she would begin to love me again. I wanted that. I longed for her affection, physically and emotionally. I was lonely and I realized in that moment of contemplating the scripture that my love was not pure, it was tainted by my desire to be loved back. That seemed human, that seemed justified and understandable, but I realized that it wasn't the pure love that was being talked about in the verses I was reading. Mine did not measure up to His for sure. I was often "seeking my own way", working my own agenda, driven by my loneliness and pain. My love had conditions. "Love me back" was perhaps the main one. God's love did not have conditions. He loved me. He loved me whether I loved Him back or not. I loved Joanne, but I desperately wanted her to love me in return and it affected how I acted toward her and how I reached out to her.

I thought about all the years before this last one. God had loved me from birth. I was unaware of that love for the most part and I did little for the first twenty-six years of my life to show my appreciation for His love, to return my love to Him. That had changed in the last year, but all those years before. There were times I remembered He was there, helping me, yet I just kept going along, not thinking about Him, not thinking about that love. I didn't know it, I didn't understand it, I had never been really taught much about it or experienced it to any great degree. Only on occasion. But He still loved me over all those years, no less than He loved me now. That love didn't depend on my reciprocation. It was there regardless. Though I knew now He always desired me to know Him, He didn't "seek His own way", in the sense that it was selfish, like mine, or dependent on my loving Him back. If I never responded back, the love would continue. Always. It was truly unconditional. I wanted my love for Joanne to be like His. Could that ever even be? I felt weak and inadequate to that task. And I was. I was incapable in myself to produce that kind of love. I began to weep. There was a heavy sense of His presence in the room as I knelt there, tears beginning to stream down my cheeks. Within me a voice seemed to speak, very clearly, not audibly, but the words and the thought were unmistakable.

"If Joanne never comes back to you, never again returned your love, would you stay committed to her? Would you be there for her, if she ever did need you and even if she didn't?"

"I don't know Lord."

"Would you remain single and be there for her if she ever turned to you for help or anything else?"

I realized in that moment that the Lord was calling me to a commitment in my marriage that truly would reflect the kind of love He had for me and her and all of us. I knew then that it meant that I would not pursue another relationship, that I would not remarry another, that I would remain faithful to Joanne even if we were no longer together. In my mind the thought came, "You're saying that I won't ever remarry unless it's to her, aren't you?"

There was a silence, but I knew the answer, even in the stillness.

"That's a hard, hard way, Lord," I said in my mind to Him. "I don't know if I can do that. I know I could never do that without Your being with me in it. If it is what you want from me in this, I will try. I will not remarry. I will not seek another. I will love Joanne, whether she loves me back or not."

I had said the words in my mind. It was what I knew the Lord wanted from me, but I knew I could never live by them without Him. In my heart, I felt that my commitment to try was honest before Him. If He would help me, I would really try to walk that walk.

I was still crying and emotional. I felt almost like I was in a cloud with Him. I became aware, in the next moment, that I was at the back of the chapel. During my conversation with the Lord, I had got up and moved to the rear of the room. I had hardly been aware of the physical movement. What was happening in my mind in that time had nearly obscured my senses. Now the room returned, quiet and peaceful and thick still with His presence. What I had just experienced was like nothing I had ever experienced before. God had taught me a personal lesson about His love. I did not think I would ever be the same. As I left the room I felt changed from the inside out. It was a teaching moment with the Lord and a challenge to commit to my marriage beyond anything I had ever envisioned.

CHAPTER 50-"A DIFFERENT KIND OF LOVE"

Winter had settled in. Snow had fallen. I spent Thanksgiving with Ted and Jeanne Hoit, a couple from the church that had been a huge support to me. Some of my friends from church, knowing and seeing the pain I was going through I think wanted me to move on so I would just stop hurting. I wore my heart on my sleeve and I may have worn some of them out as well. Not Ted and Jeanne. Their marriage had been healed and they knew what the Lord could do and stood with me in faith. Thanksgiving Day they had a houseful of people. I had a good time and noticed I wasn't as preoccupied with my situation in the conversations I had with people that day.

After the holiday, about midweek, I got a call from Joanne, asking me if I could pick up the kids for her after school and bring them home. She had an appointment with a doctor or something and couldn't be there in the afternoon. I told her I would. I thought to myself, "This wasn't my initiative here, so I ought to do this." I wanted to see Michelle and Keri. I missed them, even if it had only been a short time away from them.

I left work early and drove to the preschool to pick them up. We drove the short distance back to the apartment and I brought them upstairs. Michelle had a key and I went into the apartment with them to wait for Joanne. The kids wandered off to their room to play with something and I sat down at the kitchen table to wait.

I looked around the room at a clutter of dirty dishes in the sink and pots and pans left on the stove. I thought to myself, "Maybe I could clean this up for her, just help her out some." Part of me wanted to do this, another part of me seemed to say, "No, you don't need to do that." I got up and walked to the living room window, debating in my mind, "Should I or shouldn't I?" I looked out to the mountains you could see from the apartment. I remembered when I first came and saw this place, when we were married, how I fell in love with this view immediately. You could see the whole of the Chugach range which rose up behind Anchorage to the east, now, in late November, covered in their white coat which they would not take off until April or even May. I told Joanne we would take the place, more for the view than anything else. It seemed like an age ago that that had happened. The view was still the same, beautiful. Maybe just looking at God's hand in creation tipped the scale and I decided to do the dishes just to help. I had no other motivation that I was aware of, no alterior motive. Being the kitchen, as far as cooking and cleaning, being the least used room in any house I had lived in, it took me about an hour to finish. When I was through it looked spotless.

Almost immediately Joanne came home and I said goodbye to the girls and left. I thought as I drove away, "Before my Sunday moment in the chapel I may have hung around until she noticed what I did and looked for some response, a 'thank you' in the least." It really didn't matter this time. It was enough to have simply done it.

On the following Sunday, I came by after church to see the kids again, just to say hello for a few minutes. They were glad to see me and the four of us sat in the living room and just talked. Joanne had thanked me for cleaning up the kitchen the other day. It was pleasant. There was no tension, no arguing, and no agenda on my part to try and influence Joanne in any way toward me or the Lord. It had been a long time since we had argued about the Bible. I think, to some degree, I had finally managed to give that up, trying to convince her about Jesus. That was God's place. I was to live my life as a Christian and hopefully she would see the change in me. I knew she recognized some changes. The obvious ones were there, my appearance, the fact that I had given up drugs, my language. I wondered if she would see the deeper changes, if what had happened in the chapel, my renewed commitment to be there for her, would show through. I thought about the dishes. It was a small thing, but it was something I had done unconditionally, without any expectation of return, of a response from her. That was a different way for me. I realized that to some small degree. I wasn't "seeking my own way."

"I have to put my snow tires on sometime," Joanne said. "It's started snowing and I still don't have them on."

"You better do that soon," I said. "It's dangerous without them."

"I know," she replied

The following Wednesday, it snowed again. We left work early to wait for it to stop. You can never frame houses well, when you're packing down freshly fallen snow by walking on it. After it's packed, it turns to ice when the temperature drops. Better to wait until it has all fallen and then go back immediately and shovel off the job, while the snow is light and fluffy. I was doing my own jobs now and had guys working for me. It was early in the afternoon when I disbanded the crew and headed home.

I thought about the snow tires. On an impulse, I headed out to the apartment. She was there. "Where are your tires? I'll put them on."

She looked a little surprised, but smiled back at me warmly. "Thanks, Carl. They're in my trunk. I only have two."

"That should be all right. Give me your keys, I'll get them on before it gets dark."

She handed me the car keys and I went downstairs. It was still snowing. I got a jack from my car and crawled under the back of Joanne's to position it. When I got out from under the car, I looked up at the second-floor window, where Donna and Stan, Joanne's neighbors, lived. They had been my neighbors too when we were together. Stan was the son of the couple I had met my first day at Abbott Loop. Donna was staring at me out the window. I looked away quickly, as if I didn't see her and began loosening the lugs on the back wheels of the car. I thought that this was a timely moment. I always had believed Donna, divorced herself, may have had an influence initially, when we first separated. She may have thought, that like her own ex-husband, a year and a half after our separation, I would be long gone. As she looked down, watching me crawl around under Joanne's car in the snow, I imagined she might be thinking, "He is either really nuts, or he really loves Joanne." I wondered as I finished changing the tires. I didn't look back up at the window to see if she was still there.

When I was done, I went back upstairs to give Joanne her keys back. She had made some hot chocolate and the girls came out and we sat together and sipped at the steaming cups. The girls were teasing each other and laughing. Joanne and I sat there silently for a moment.

"Why don't we go out to dinner Saturday night? Do

you want to?" I asked.

Joanne hesitated for a moment and then said, "Okay."

I was dumbfounded, but managed to reply, "I'll pick you up around six o'clock."

"All right, " Joanne said.

I left a few minutes later. Since the chapel experience a lot was different. I was seeing her more now than I had in months and now we were going on a date. I knew something had changed with me since that day in the church. Did Joanne see it when I cleaned the kitchen and changed her tires? Such seemingly insignificant things, yet maybe the Lord was using them. Asking her out just came out spontaneously. I wasn't pushing anything. I was at peace and obviously thrilled with her reply as much as I had ever been since this all started. Did she notice something different?

CHAPTER 51-"THE DATE"

I spent Saturday cleaning my car inside and out, making it as spotless as I could. I had made reservations at the Anchorage Westward downtown, the classiest hotel in town. They had a restaurant on the top floor with a view. I called and told Joanne where we were going. I would wear a suit and try to look sharp.

I picked her up at six and drove downtown to the hotel. Our reservations were for seven. We kind of small-talked along the way. I could tell we were both a little tense. I was determined not to bring up any sensitive issues in our conversation, church or such, but just try and show her a nice time, be a gentleman and all that. I told her about work, we talked about Michelle and Keri, what good kids they were, about news we had from Massachusetts. We maneuvered around all the flash-points pretty well.

The food was good and expensive. I paid the bill and we drove home quietly, small-talking still. I took her upstairs to the apartment and came in and sat down for a few moments. I wanted to kiss her goodnight. I felt like that would be pushing things. She looked beautiful as always, her brown eyes like deep pools lying still along a quiet stream. All night we had looked into each other's eyes, with affection I had hoped. I said goodnight and left clumsily. We had survived the night though without a misunderstanding. A couple of times in our conversation we had come close, but I had consciously refrained from pursuing sensitive subjects. I felt good about that. I left wondering what would come next. Was this a start? I had no idea what she was feeling. I pictured her lying in bed and wondered what she was thinking as I drove home.

CHAPTER
52-"BREAKTHROUGH"

I had told the girls that I would take them ice-skating at Jewel Lake on Sunday, so after church I headed over to the apartment. Michelle and Keri were excited and ready to go. Joanne was there alone, so I asked her if she wanted to go with us. She said she would, so we all headed out to the lake together. I was amazed at all the opportunities that suddenly seemed to be presenting themselves for us to be together.

When we got to the frozen lake I laced up the girls' skates while Joanne put her's on and the three of them went out on the ice while I put on mine. When I was done I joined them. Joanne, Michelle and Keri all were huddled together on the ice, the girls taking steps hesitantly and usually falling after each one. I skated up to them and stopped beside them. I said to Joanne, "Hey, you look familiar, weren't we married at one time? We had a couple of kids too, didn't we? Are these them?" My poor attempt at humor but Joanne laughed. I had broken the ice, no pun intended. We each took one of the girls by the hand and made our way around the cleared portion of the lake slowly. We were all together. To anyone looking on, we looked like the most normal of families. I had to pinch myself. This was really happening. We hadn't been this close in a year-and- a-half. We spent a couple of hours' skating until we were all a little wet from spending more time on our butts than our feet, and cold from the falling temperatures in the twilight of the day.

We drove back to the apartment shivering. By the time the heater began making a difference in my car, we were there.

"Hot chocolate, hot chocolate, mom," the girls cried.

"Do you want some?" Joanne asked.

"Sure," I replied and we headed upstairs.

We took our boots off and left them in the hall. Joanne went to the kitchen and began making the chocolate. I laid on the living room floor and the girls started jumping on me. Still dressed in all our outdoor clothes, we rolled around on the floor like furballs. Michelle and Keri were laughing hysterically. Michelle was loosening up with me a lot more than I had seen her do in weeks. She smiled and laughed as she ran across the room and jumped with abandon onto my stomach. "Hop on pop". I tickled her as best I could through her winter coat. She was having so much fun with me. I didn't know whether to laugh or cry. I noticed Joanne watching us from the kitchen. It was a pleasant scene that our living room hadn't experienced in some time.

"Michelle, Keri, take your snowsuits off and come to

the kitchen. Your chocolate is ready," Joanne said.

They peeled themselves off of me and I helped Keri pull off her snowsuit. Michelle came up to me and sat down in front of me. "Daddy, help me."

"Okay, stand up.". I unzipped the top, pulled it down and lightly shoved her over on her behind. She giggled. I pulled the suit off her legs and she ran off to the kitchen where Keri was already seated at the table.

"I can make you coffee," Joanne offered.

"Hot chocolate is okay," I replied.

I was standing at the window, looking at the remains of the day. The mountains in the distance were a deep purple-blue, the last remnant of color against the deepening gray skyline at their peaks. It was a cold wintry look. Above the tree-line the white of the snow on the rocky summits was everywhere present.

"There isn't anytime of year that you can't look out at those mountains and see something beautiful looking back at you is there," I said?

"No, we live in a low rent district with a high rent view," she said.

"As soon as I looked out this window, I wanted this place," I replied.

"I remember," Joanne said.

We sat together on the coach and sipped at our cups. It was quiet, the only sound the constant chatter of the girls from the kitchen. Joanne turned on a couple of lamps. It was dark now outside. She sat back down on the couch next to me, but not close. I didn't kiss her after our date the other night. I wanted to reach out and touch her now, but it wouldn't have been right I thought to myself. I felt it though. I wondered if she felt something toward me then.

That morning at church they had announced that Mike Premo was going to share his testimony about how he came to the Lord. He would do it tonight at the evening service. Mike had had a rough younger life. Been in prison. His story was a moving one. He was a changed man.

I thought about asking Joanne to go. I hesitated. Would I be going back to the same old pattern of pushing things? The last two weeks had been so good I wasn't sure.

Joanne got up, "I'm going to go take off some of these wet clothes," she said, "I'll be back."

She left me to my pondering. I waited a few minutes. The girls were preoccupied at the kitchen table. I headed back toward the bedroom. The door was opened and Joanne was standing at her mirror and combing her hair.

"Can I come in?" I asked.

"What for?"

"Don't worry," I said and sat down on the edge of the bed. The light was soft in the room. "Joanne, come to church with me tonight. A guy is telling his story. how he came to know Jesus. That's all. Just listen to it, see what you think."

She hesitated for a moment, still looking into the mirror. I couldn't see the expression on her face from where I was sitting. "I don't think so," she replied finally.

"Joanne, please, just listen and see what happens. See how you feel. It's not my story. It's his. The results are the same, but how he gets there is different. He had a tough life. Broken homes. You know what that is."

Again, a hesitation, "No, I don't want to, " she repeated.

I hung my head in my hands. "Why can't you just go and see? I don't understand."

"I don't think I need this," she countered.

"Everyone does. You want peace, fulfillment? I know you do. This is it. It's what we've been looking for all these years of pot-smoking, acid-dropping, hitch-hiking. Jesus is it? It's what was missing. Why doesn't anyone believe me? When I was writing songs back in Massachusetts everyone seemed to hang on *every word like I knew what I was talking about or had some answers. I knew nothing. Now I know something and nobody wants to listen."*

"It's your way, not mine," she replied.

"God gave it to all of us. It's not supposed to be just for some," I countered back. We were beginning to argue, here I was doing it again. The volume of our voices was rising.

"I don't think it's for me," she hurled back as she turned and left the room.

Again, I hung my head. We hadn't done this in so long. I hadn't pushed it on her. I didn't want to do this. Why did I let myself go now? This will ruin everything that's been accomplished in the last two weeks. I looked around the room, got up off the bed and began almost pacing. I ached. I left the room, heading back down the hallway to the living room. She was sitting dejectedly on the couch. "I'm sorry Joanne, I didn't mean to do this. I'm sorry."

She sat silently for a moment. "It always ends this way, doesn't it? I don't think it will ever change Carl."

"I should leave now." I walked over to the girls and hugged them, trying to hold back tears. It seemed hopeless to me at this moment. Maybe she wouldn't come to know the Lord after all. Michelle looked up at me with a sad look in her eyes, as if she knew something was wrong. I turned and walked to the door. I hugged the girls. "Goodbye," I said feebly and

left.

The door closed behind me. I slipped on my boots that were lying outside the door and almost staggered down the stairs and out into the chill, frozen air of the Alaskan night. It cut through me like an unyielding knife. So cold, I thought it would freeze my tears. How many tears I had shed over the last year-and-a-half. I had never cried so much in my life. Some were tears of sadness, some were tears of joy. I had run the gauntlet of emotions. Tonight's were tears of anger and frustration. Anger at myself, anger at the Lord, like it was somehow His fault I had blown it. I got into my car and without looking, backed out and into the main lane of the parking spaces, heading away from my family for what I thought might really be a final time.

"Why did You let this happen," I cried? "Why didn't You do something to stop me? I've ruined everything, maybe for good."

I pulled up to the end of the row of apartments and stopped to look for traffic before I turned out onto the frontage road that led out to the highway. I heard the distinct sensation of a voice within me say, "Go back."

I don't know if I spoke audibly or in my mind next. "What," I questioned? "Go back?" I had the sense that the voice was the Holy Spirit's though.

"That sounds crazy. Really? How can I do that," I questioned again?

"Go back," again.

I felt like beating my head against the steering wheel. In a kind of daze I backed up and turned around, drove back to where I had parked and ascended once again the stairway to the apartment. I knocked. I could hear her moving toward the door from the other side.

"Who is it?" she asked.

"It's me," I replied.

She opened the door. We stood staring at each other for an awkward moment. "Joanne, I don't even know what I'm doing here, but...," my voice trailed off.

"Come in," she said.

I took two steps into the living room. "Joanne, come with me tonight." It must have been like the plaintive cry of one of God's creatures in the wilderness, from the mountains in the distance which had now faded into the night.

"All right, I will," she replied.

CHAPTER 53-"SALVATION"

We arrived at the church at around five forty-five. Joanne had left the kids downstairs with Donna. The service was going to begin at six o'clock. We found a seat near the back, in the center section, on the left-hand side. We sat down. I could not find anything to say, no small talk, in the fifteen minutes before the service started. Some people began to come by and say hello. I introduced Joanne to everyone that did. I had the feeling that the news that she was there spread throughout the building in a flash. Everyone knew my situation and many had been praying for her. I hoped that word would spread to the prayer chapel, where many in the congregation were praying now for the service that was about to happen. Vince came by. He was all smiles and cheerfully greeted Joanne. I saw him head toward the chapel right after saying hello. I knew that by the time church began, probably everyone would know that Joanne was here with me, maybe even Mike Premo, who was preaching.

At six the ministers came in and took seats on the stage in front. Three sat there, Mike Premo, Jim Brenn and Dick Strutz.

The service started off as usual with singing. There

was really a rather small crowd I thought for the occasion. Mike was popular in the congregation and a good speaker. I had expected more might be here than the five or six hundred that were. But not many churches in the area could draw that number on a Sunday morning, much less a Sunday night.

The worship service was short. The choir had taken their places on stage and did a couple of songs. Vince was in the choir. He looked in my direction a number of times. I could see his eyes shift our way. After their songs, the choir remained seated in the front and Mike came to the pulpit.

He introduced himself and began to tell the story of his life. His early years were in a broken home. He stayed with his father, moving from place to place in the South, mostly in Florida and Georgia. He was in and out of trouble all the time, in and out of youth authorities, in and out of jails and prison. He had come west to try to put his past behind him, get a fresh start. He was married and had a family but got into more trouble in Seattle dealing dope. He was arrested again and released on bail pending his trial. He had moved up to Alaska in the interim and it was here that he met the Lord. His trial had been delayed some time and Mike became involved in ministry and preaching while he waited to go back to Seattle. He came on staff at Abbott Loop as an evangelist and when he finally went back to Seattle and faced the judge, his case was dismissed. The judge was sufficiently impressed at the change in his life and because of his visible rehabilitation, dropped all the charges against him and he returned to Alaska and his family and the church with a clean slate. I am not sure he even expected that. It was a highpoint in the recent history of Abbott Loop and Mike was a large part of the ministry of the church today.

His story was an impressive one. The Lord had changed everything in his life. It was obvious in hearing him relate it. I wondered as I sat there how Joanne was reacting to it. I hadn't said a word to her throughout the service, wasn't trying to influence her in any way. She was listening intently, I could tell that.

When Mike finished, he gave an altar call. He invited people to come and turn their hearts to the Lord. He said that the change in him could be the change in them if they would ask Jesus to be a part of their lives. Some of the musicians who had played during the worship service had gone back on-stage. When Mike had finished his invitation, he asked people who wanted to respond to come to the front of the church and he would go with them to another room outside and explain more about the step they were taking and pray with them there.

He stepped off the stage and stood in the open space in front of it and waited. Jim Brenn came to the pulpit and asked the musicians to play "Amazing Grace" and the congregation to stand and sing quietly as people searched their thoughts and hearts and hopefully "made their decisions for Jesus".

I bowed my head and closed my eyes. I waited, hoping for some response from Joanne. Nothing happened. My emotions were a tangle, but I refrained from saying anything to her. It was her decision, it was in God's hand. I didn't even look in her direction. I had no idea how all this was affecting her.

I don't know if what Jim did next was motivated by the Lord or because he knew Joanne was in the congregation. I'm sure she wasn't the only one he was thinking of but I knew that he knew she was there. He said, "I want to play this song again. There may be some of you out there who are on the fence between coming forward and staying in your seat. I want to give you some more time to think about this. Jesus is here. Come to Him." The musicians began playing "Amazing Grace" one more time. The choir began singing the words in the background. I had not sung them either time. My head was bowed in prayer.

I could hear the words now filling the room. (Amazing grace, how sweet the sound) "Lord," I was thinking the thoughts of a prayer to Him as the melody could be heard around us, "I remember that dream you gave me." (that saved a wretch like me) "I saw Joanne in a church going to the altar to accept You." (I once was lost) "I believe that that dream was from you." (but now am found) "I want to see that happen Jesus, (was blind, but now I see) now."

My head was still bowed, my eyes were still closed.

Carl Gove

As soon as I thought the word "now" in my prayer, I felt a tap on my shoulder. It was Joanne. I opened my eyes and looked at her. She looked back and said, "I want to go down there, take me with you."

We made our way to the aisle. My arm was around her as we walked forward. My head was lowered slightly, as was hers. We were holding on to each other slowly moving forward down the aisle. I saw the carpet at my feet, my navy blue Pendleton shirt. As I reached across my body to hold her I felt as though we were stumbling and bumbling along, on our way to the front of the church, toward Jesus. Other than the two of us I was unaware of what was happening in the room. I couldn't hear anything anymore. If they were playing another verse of the hymn I didn't know it. I didn't look anywhere but ahead at the floor, trying to steady myself and her.

We made it to the front and stood there with others that had come. I looked up then and ahead, not at Jim or Mike. My eyes focused beyond them to the large cross that hung on the wall behind the stage, behind the choir. When everyone who was coming forward had arrived, we left the room.

The time came for Joanne to pray. This was not part of the dream I had had. In none of my imaginings of how my wife would come to the Lord, did I see myself there with her, standing next to her, hearing her voice, holding her hand, as she gave her life to Jesus. I thought of a scripture that talks about how

God answers prayer. It says, "exceeding, abundantly, above all we ask or think". This was that for me. I could hear Mike as he led the group and I could hear Joanne repeating after him, "Lord Jesus, I realize tonight that I'm a sinner, that I've fallen short of Your plans for my life. Forgive me Lord, come into my life tonight and change me and help me to walk with You from this day on. Amen."

CHAPTER 54-"RECONCILED"

Three weeks had passed. We stood in the back of the sanctuary at the beginning of the center aisle. The evening service had just ended. Nine hundred to a thousand people were in the auditorium.

"Are you ready?" I asked.

"Yes, " Joanne replied.

She was dressed in a long, flowered dress that reached to the floor. The color was white with delicate orange floral designs in it. Her hair hung over her shoulders and down almost to her waist. A single white rose was pinned in it, high on her forehead and to one side. We looked at each other and smiled. I had bought a suit for the occasion, and wore an orange shirt that nearly matched the orange in her gown. Michelle and Keri had new dresses, white with blue flowers and turquoise waistbands. They each had a bouquet of flowers, as did Joanne.

The music began. I held Joanne's hand and Keri's, who was on my other side. Michelle was on Joanne's side. Jim Brenn waited for us at the front of the church, up on the stage, below the cross that hung on the wall. We walked down the aisle and up the steps to the altar where we all stood before Jim.

He began the service, "The Bible says that 'he who finds a wife, finds a good thing and receives blessing from the Lord. Carl, it's apparent to all here tonight, seeing Joanne, that this is true."

Soon, we turned and faced each other and looked in each other's eyes, as we had done almost seven years before. Love was still there, and now, Jesus was too. Neither of us looked to the right or the left.

"Carl, do you take this woman to be your wife.? "

"I do."

"Joanne, do you take this man to be your husband?"

"I do."

We took communion to remember Jesus. We hadn't done that in our first marriage.

Finally Jim said, "I now pronounce you man and wife, again."

I kissed my bride.

The ministers and elders of the church came and gathered around all of us, Michelle and Keri included. Joanne and I knelt on the carpet facing the cross. The girls seemed lost amongst all the hands that reached out toward us and were laid upon our shoulders and heads, to bless us and our union. Dick Benjamin prayed for us and then Tom Edmunson did too. At the end of Tom's prayer, he pronounced, "God has done this for you, and for His glory."

Reconciled. A new beginning.

EPILOGUE

Everything you have read is true to the best of my recollection. Some of the details were clearer than others, but all these things did happen. Truth is better than fiction I believe in this story.

It has been fifty-one years now since the events of this book occurred. We have two more children and eight grandchildren. Michelle and Keri are both married now. The Lord has continued to bless our lives.

Our story was told from my point of view. Joanne has her story too. In the three weeks that followed the service where she gave her life to the Lord, we had some ups and downs. God continued to be there in remarkable ways for us. At one point, Joanne really didn't know what she should do, whether she should remarry me or not. She was at the apartment by herself and prayed to the Lord for direction. Randomly opening her Bible, which was in front of her, her eyes fell on this verse: "If a woman leaves her husband, let her remain unmarried or be reconciled to him." (from Romans 7) Kind of like the situation I had experienced in Haines, after I had spoken in tongues. God met her there and showed her His Way.

I found a place to rent in the foothills outside of Anchorage. A small house built into the side of a hill, with large windows on the front and side. We could sit in the living room and watch the kids slide by in the snow during winter. It had a mailbox in front, with our name on it. We were a family again, a family who knew Jesus.

The scene at the church the night Joanne gave her life to the Lord, when we came down the aisle together, I was told afterwards, was electric. Some said they felt God's presence fill the room like a wind had blown through. The Lord put us on display that night, for everyone there to see. Our situation gave the church a lift spiritually that lasted for some time. A good friend of mine, who was there that night, was reunited with his wife six months later. During our times of separation from our wives we had developed a close kinship. We understood each other's pain and hope in Jesus as well as anyone could. Joanne had a part in leading his wife to the Lord. We stood as their witnesses in a private wedding ceremony in Tom Edmunson's office. We are still close friends today.

We all know that divorce has attacked our world like the plague. It has devastated marriages both in and out of the church. We found that God cared about Joanne and I and about our marriage. He became real to us and showed us, in the most personal ways, who He was. Our hopes are that our story can help you find Him in your lives, as individuals, and in your marriages, as husbands and wives.

Divorce is not the only problem that Jesus can affect in our lives. I often say that "I found what I was looking for when I found the Lord." I meant that I found inner peace, purpose and direction and an understanding of the "scheme of things". We all have those desires, to know "why we're here", "what it all means". I think that is what "being created in His image" is all about. The desire to know Him, to know truth, is bred into us by God, the One who made us. Jesus is the way to understand it all, the way to finally sense that connection to the meaning of life, to God Himself. I started this book with a quote from scripture and I finish it with the same quote: "Be reconciled to God." (1st Corinthians 5:20) Because Joanne and I were reconciled to Him we were able to be reconciled to each other. Ask Him to reveal Himself to you as He did to us. It will happen. I guarantee it, but more importantly, He does.

"Ask, and it will be given to you; seek, and you will find; knock, and it will be opened to you. For everyone who asks receives, and he who seeks finds and to him who knocks it will be opened." Matthew 7:7-8

A final word. My story with the Lord, which you have read, is an account of my personal experiences with Him. I had been raised in a Christian church and knew God as the One the Bible teaches of and knew in fact, but not experience, that Jesus was His Son. I had heard the words 'sin', 'Heaven', 'Hell', 'forgiveness', 'salvation', 'Baptism', and 'Communion' growing up; even went through the rituals of formal Baptism as a child and Communion in many Sunday morning services, but had no real understanding of the spiritual meaning of these terms or practices. So when my life was turned around pounding nails on that deck in Haines, I was a neophyte in regard to what Scripture taught.

Now I understand that I am a sinner, weakened in my very nature, doing wrong things before God and therefore separated in relationship from Him by that wrongdoing. It started with everyone's grandfather and grandmother, Adam and Eve. They were judged when they disobeyed God, when they sinned, and ate of the forbidden fruit. Mankind fell from a perfect state and was removed from a perfect place. Like our ancient grandparents, in my life I too had sinned and disobeyed God's commands. We all have, and because God is just and holy, I was under His judgment for that wrongdoing. The judgment of sin is death, not just physical death, but spiritual death as well and it is for eternity. There is a Hell to pay for continued, willful, rejection of God. Some would like to waterdown statements like that, but you really can't.

My sin necessitated a punishment and I had to come

to grips with that. God loved me, but I was not okay before Him and nothing I could do on my own could cleanse me permanently. I needed help, some way to save me from sin's effect. I was lost, but God did not leave me in my helpless condition but came to earth Himself in the flesh, just like us. And Jesus, without sin and being God, took the punishment I deserved when He went to the Cross. The just judgment God required Jesus took on Himself, dying the most horrible of deaths by crucifixion. God's love and justice were both displayed that day. Christ satisfied justice by taking the penalty for my sin. When He died in my place, my judgment for my sins died with Him. His love for me was demonstrated to the fullest. He provided the permanent remedy for sin that I could never provide for myself.

Judgment and mercy kissed that day at Calvary and three days later Jesus was raised from a garden tomb. Death could not hold Him; because of that Resurrection I was raised to a whole new life. I know today that the Cross and the Resurrection are at the very heart of all that the Bible teaches, that God, in Christ Jesus, came to save us, to die in our place at the Cross and to give us new life in His Resurrection. This is the Gospel, the "Good News". Therein is life forever if we believe on Him, on Jesus Christ.

"For God so loved the world that He gave His only begotten Son, that whoever believes in Him should not perish but have everlasting life." John 3:16

There is a Heaven to gain.

This may all sound like a Billy Graham sermon to some. Nothing wrong with that, but it isn't. It is my best attempt to share Christ's Gospel. I knew little of these things when I had that initial experience in Haines. It is the theology and doctrine I did not understand back then, but what I have come to learn since from the Bible. What I did on the floor of that hotel room that morning was I turned to Him and humbly cried out for Him to show me who He is, and He did. I turned to God and He came close, closer than I ever knew He could be.

That is what I hope can be a takeaway for you from my story. Turn to God, the God of the Bible. It is His desire for all of us. He wants to show Himself to us and become real in our lives. so we will know Him. He will take us from our turning, forgive our sins, cleanse us, and teach us His ways, about who Jesus is, about the Cross, the Resurrection, the Holy Spirit, about all the things that pertain to a life with Him! God has done His part in the relationship by coming into this world, as Jesus, when we were lost spiritually. Our part is to believe that He is here and that He will hear and answer humble and sincere prayers that come from our hearts to Him. From my story and the stories of every 'born-again' Christian alive, from the stories that the Bible tells of God and man's interactions throughout our histories, believe! These are some of the greatest stories ever told. This one has been mine and Joanne's.

Made in the USA
Middletown, DE
24 September 2022

10831834R00166